INTRODUCTION TO FLIPPING PROPERTIES

THE REAL ESTATE INVESTING
MENTOR
THE AFFORDABLE $50K COACHING ALTERNATIVE

James Orr
The Real Estate Financial Planner™

© Copyright 2024 by James Orr. All rights reserved. This book, or parts thereof, may not be reproduced in any form without permission from the publisher; exceptions are made for brief excerpts used in published reviews.

Published by:

Real Estate Financial Planner LLC
PO Box 2163
Loveland CO 80539

https://RealEstateFinancialPlanner.com

First edition November 2024.
File: 2024-11-13 - Introduction to Flipping Properties

This publication is designed to provide accurate and authoritative information regarding the subject matter covered. It is sold with the understanding that the publisher is not engaged in rendering legal, accounting or other professional advice or services. If legal advice or other expert advice is required, the services of a competent professional person should be sought.

From a *Declaration of Principles* jointly adopted by a Committee of American Bar Association and a Committee of Publishers and Associations.

This is a work of fiction. References to clients in this book are fictional and have been modified and changed from any possible real situations to protect the identities of clients and to simplify the stories for clarity. In some cases, significant parts of the stories have been changed. In some cases, stories have been completely fabricated to illustrate a concept. Any similarities to people alive or dead is purely coincidental.

AI Disclosure: While James Orr authored the original version of this content, AI was used extensively to draft, proofread, edit, improve and write subsequent versions and variations.

DEDICATION

Dedicated to my wife Tammy. I have no words.

FREE DOWNLOAD

The World's Greatest Real Estate Deal Analysis Spreadsheet™

Thank you for purchasing this book and taking the next step toward mastering real estate investing.

As a special bonus, you can download *The World's Greatest Real Estate Deal Analysis Spreadsheet*™ for free. This powerful tool will help you analyze deals like a pro, ensuring you make informed, profitable decisions.

Download your free copy now and start running the numbers with confidence.

https://REFP.com/spreadsheet

© 2024 James Orr. All rights reserved.

Table of Contents

Introduction to Flipping Properties 1
   Flipping Properties 1
   Flipping Variations 2
   Financing Flipping Properties 3
      Most Common Financing 3
      More Unusual Methods 4
   Active or Passive 6
   Duration 7
   Exit 8
   Exit Channels 8
   Exit Financing 9
   Investor/Entrepreneur 10
   Money Required 12
   Credit Required 14
   Skills Required 15
   Stability 17
   Scalability 18
   Risk Exposure 19
   Profit Speed 21
   Finding Deals 23
      Most Common Methods 23
      More Unusual Methods 25

Searching for Fixer Upper Deals 26
Analyzing Deals 28
Market Conditions 29
    Ideal 29
    Challenging 30
Accessibility/Availability 30
Using Retirement Account 32
1 Rental = 1 Flip/Year 33

Introduction to Real Estate Deal Analysis 36
Download Spreadsheet for Free 37
Spreadsheet Inputs 38
    Purchase Inputs 38
    Mortgage Inputs 40
    Monthly Income 41
    Annual Expenses 41
    Depreciation Details 42
Overrides 43
Dashboard 44
    Monthly Cash Flow - Year 1 45
    Return in Dollars - Year 1 45
    Return on Investment - Year 1 46
    Returns if Sold (ROI and IRR) 48
    Cash on Cash ROI & Cap Rate - Years 1-5 48
    Return on True Net Equity™ 49
    Annual Key Metrics - Year 1 50

© 2024 James Orr. All rights reserved.

Annual Non-Loan Expenses - Year 1	51
Equities and Cost-To-Access	52
94 Ways to Improve Cash Flow on Rental Properties	54
7 Distinct Real Estate Investing Stages for Improving Cash Flow	55
Searching for Properties	56
Financing the Property	61
Before Getting Loan	61
Pay Upfront Instead of Financing	62
Change/Improve Borrower(s)	63
Relationship With Lender	64
Change Amortization	64
Loan Terms	65
Private Mortgage Insurance (PMI)	66
Other Properties	67
Non-Traditional Financing	68
Improving the Real Estate Investing Strategy	70
Improving the Property	73
Marketing the Property for Rent	75
While Owning the Property	77
Refi/Pay Off Loan	77
Taxes	78
Insurance	78
Making Payments	79
Management	80

© 2024 James Orr. All rights reserved.

Maintenance	81
Depreciation	81
While Renting the Property	82
Add Services	82
Charge Appropriately	82
Convenience Billing	83
Timing	84
Miscellaneous	85
Conclusion	85
Introduction to Monte Carlo Analysis of Rental Properties	87
Not Just Property Appreciation	90
Does This Even Matter?	91
Monte Carlo Modeling	93
What If They Became Homeowners Instead of Renting?	95
Buying Rental Properties with 20% Down Payments	96
Owner-Occupant, Rentals and Stocks	100
Nomad™ Real Estate Investing Strategy Example	101
Additional Modeling	103
Not Just Financial Independence	105
About the Author	134
A Small Request	136
Questions?	137

© 2024 James Orr. All rights reserved.

Introduction to Flipping Properties

Flipping properties, at its core, involves purchasing undervalued properties, renovating them to increase their market value, and selling them for a profit.

It is a real estate investing strategy that generates short-term profits.

Flipping Properties

Flipping properties typically consists of the following 3 steps:

- **Buy Properties** - You begin with finding undervalued properties. Often these properties need work, but the value can sometimes be solving a seller's problem that does not involve fixing up the property itself.
- **Add Value** - Renovate, upgrade, or make strategic improvements to increase the property's worth.

- **Resell Properties** - Once you've boosted the property's value, it's time to sell. Your goal is to sell quickly and for a profit.

Flipping Variations

There are several variations of flipping properties you can explore, each with its unique advantages.

Here's a breakdown of the main variations:

- **Traditional Flipping** - This is the classic "fix and flip" approach. You buy a property that needs some TLC, renovate it quickly, and sell it for a profit.
- **Live-in Flips** - Want to save on living expenses while flipping? You move into the property and work on renovations in your spare time. It's like having a second job, but you're building sweat equity in your own home.
- **2-Year Tax-Advantaged Live-In Flips** - This is a slower approach with potential tax benefits. You live in the property for at least two years while making improvements. When you sell, you will likely avoid capital gains tax on the profit. However, the modeling I've done suggests you'll do better financially in many cases by paying taxes and doing more frequent flips.
- **Seller Partnership Flips** – Seller Partnership Flips involve collaborating with the property seller to increase profitability. This strategy allows investors to leverage the seller's existing ownership (and financing) to potentially reduce upfront costs while sharing the benefits of the flip.

Financing Flipping Properties

So, how do you finance the business of flipping properties?

Here are some of the most common financing strategies along with some of the less common, more unusual methods.

Most Common Financing

Let's explore the most common financing methods:

- **Hard Money Loans** - These are short-term loans from lenders who are in the business of making loans against real estate. They typically have higher interest rates and fees but offer quick funding. Some may look primarily to the property as collateral and rely less on the financial strength of the borrower. For traditional flips, hard money can provide fast capital for purchases and renovations. Most hard money lenders will not fund live-in flips because of the additional rules and regulations of making loans to owner-occupants. But many live-in flippers will choose to utilize low/nothing down owner-occupant financing anyway.
- **Private Money** - This involves borrowing from individuals you know, like friends or family, who are not typically in the business of making loans. It's often more flexible than hard money and may offer better terms. For traditional flips, private money can offer lower rates than hard money. In live-in flips, you might use private money for renovations after securing traditional

© 2024 James Orr. All rights reserved.

financing for the purchase. For 2-year tax-advantaged flips, private money could provide patient capital for the longer hold.
- **Cash** - Using your own cash to buy flips gives you the most flexibility but ties up your capital. For traditional flips, cash allows for quick closes and no interest costs. With live-in flips, you might use cash for the down payment and renovations. For 2-year tax-advantaged flips, cash can reduce holding costs over the longer period. In partnership flips with the seller, your cash might be used for the repairs.

More Unusual Methods

While hard money loans and private money are common financing methods for flips, there are some less conventional approaches you might consider. These options can offer flexibility and potentially better terms in certain situations.

Let's explore a few of these alternatives:

- **Traditional Owner-Occupant Financing** - This method is primarily used for *Live-in Flips* and *2-Year Tax-Advantaged Live-In Flips*. You can access lower interest rates and down payments, but you'll need to occupy the property as your primary residence. And, the property will need to be in a condition that allows for traditional financing—the most distressed properties usually won't usually qualify for traditional financing (including owner-occupant or non-owner-occupant/investor loans).

- **Traditional Non-Owner-Occupant Financing** - While less common for flips due to longer approval times, this option can work for *Traditional Flipping* if you have a longer timeline and strong credit. It often requires a larger down payment (usually 20-25%) but may offer better interest rates than hard money increasing profitability. However, lenders might not like making short term loans of this nature and the lender may be penalized if you pay off the loan in less than 6 months or 12 months.
- **Utilize Seller's Ownership** - This approach is specific to *Seller Partnership Flips*. You partner with the property owner, leveraging their existing ownership and financing on the property to reduce your upfront costs. It's an excellent way to enter the market with less capital, but requires stronger negotiation skills.
- **Creative Financing** - This umbrella term covers various strategies like owner financing, wrap financing/subject to, loan assumptions, the rent-to-own family including lease-options, and the agreement-for-deed family of financing. These methods can be applied to any flip variation. They often require less upfront capital but may involve slightly more complex negotiations and often require you to do marketing to find motivated/flexible sellers.
- **Partner with Others** - Teaming up with non-seller partners can help you access more capital or expertise. This method can be used in any flip variation, allowing you to possibly take on larger projects and/or multiple flips simultaneously. However, it requires clear

© 2024 James Orr. All rights reserved.

communication and well-defined partnership agreements.

Active or Passive

When it comes to real estate investing strategies, flipping properties is undoubtedly one of the most active approaches you can take. Unlike buy-and-hold strategies that allow for more passive income, flipping requires your constant attention and hands-on involvement.

Let's break down the activity levels of different flipping variations:

- **Traditional Flipping** - This is the most intensive variation. You're actively involved in finding deals, managing renovations, and selling properties quickly. Especially serially flipping properties, it's a full-time job that demands your undivided attention.
- **Live-in Flips** - While still active, this approach allows you to spread the work over a longer period. You're living in the property while making improvements, which can reduce the pressure to finish quickly.
- **2-Year Tax-Advantaged Live-In Flips** - This variation offers the most extended timeline, allowing you to pace your renovations over at least two years. It's less frantic than traditional flipping but still requires consistent effort.
- **Seller Partnership Flips** - By partnering with the seller, you might simplify and optimize some of the financing and expenses, but it's still an active strategy. You'll need to manage the partnership and oversee the

flip process and communicate with your partner, the seller.

Remember, while flipping can be lucrative, it's not a "set it and forget it" strategy. You're trading time for potentially higher returns. If you're looking for a more hands-off approach, you might want to consider other real estate investing strategies. However, if you're ready to roll up your sleeves and dive in, flipping could be an exciting and rewarding path for you.

Duration

When flipping properties, typically you'll hold onto the property for about 3 to 6 months. Sometimes a little shorter. Sometimes a little longer.

This timeframe allows you to purchase, renovate, and sell the property for a profit without tying up your capital for too long.

However, it's important to note that this timeline can vary depending on market conditions, the extent of renovations needed, and your specific strategy. Some flips might take longer, especially if you encounter unexpected issues or if the market slows down.

For live-in flips, your holding period will naturally be extended. You'll likely stay in the property for at least a year, both to satisfy owner-occupant financing requirements and to spread out the renovation work. This approach can be less stressful and more cost-effective, as you're not racing against the clock.

© 2024 James Orr. All rights reserved.

If you're considering a *2-Year Tax-Advantaged Live-In Flip*, you're looking at an even longer holding period. By living in the property for at least two years, you may qualify for significant capital gains tax benefits when you sell. While this strategy requires more patience, it can potentially lead to you keeping more of your profits due to the tax savings.

However, as I mentioned earlier, consider the math comparing how much you save on taxes versus how much you could make by doing more frequent flips. You may find that you'll net more money doing more frequent flips than you'd net saving some money on taxes.

Exit

Let's consider exiting your flips.

How do you typically sell the properties? In other words, what channels do you typically use?

And, what type of financing are your buyers typically using?

Exit Channels

When it's time to sell your flip, you have a couple of main channels to choose from. Let's explore your options:

- **Multiple Listing Service (MLS)** - This is the go-to method for most flippers. By listing your property on the MLS, you're exposing it to a vast network of real estate agents and potential buyers. It casts the widest net and usually gives you the largest exposure which tends to

result in maximizing your sales price in a reasonable amount of time.
- **For Sale By Owner (FSBO)** - If you're feeling confident in your sales skills, you might consider selling the property yourself. This approach can save you money on real estate agent commissions, but it requires more time and effort on your part.

Exit Financing

When you're ready to sell your flipped property, understanding the financing options available to your potential buyers is important.

Here's what you need to know:

- **Traditional Owner-Occupant Loans** - These are perfect for buyers who plan to live in the property. They often come with lower down payments and better interest rates, making your property more accessible to a wider range of buyers. Options include 3% first time home buyer conventional mortgages, 5% conventional mortgages, 3.5% down FHA loans, nothing down USDA loans for rural properties, and nothing down VA loans for eligible veterans.
- **Traditional Non-Owner-Occupant Loans** - If you're selling to an investor, they'll likely use these loans. They typically require higher down payments (often 20-25% but as low as 15% down) and come with slightly higher interest rates.
- **Cash** - Some buyers might offer to purchase your property with cash. While this can lead to a quicker,

smoother transaction, cash buyers often expect a discount on the purchase price and in most cases, flippers are trying to maximize their sale price to net the most they can.

It's important to note that if you've purchased a property and are selling it for a much higher price in a short time frame, there may be limitations on the financing your buyers can use. Some lenders have "seasoning" requirements, which means the property needs to be owned for a certain period before it can be resold—especially resold for higher prices than you bought it for. This is to prevent fraudulent flipping schemes.

For example, FHA loans typically require that a property be owned for at least 90 days before it can be resold. If you're selling within this timeframe, your pool of potential buyers might be limited to those using conventional or cash financing.

Understanding these financing options by talking to your lender can help you better prepare for the sale of your flipped property and potentially expand your pool of potential buyers.

Investor/Entrepreneur

When it comes to real estate, there's an important distinction between Real Estate Investing and Real Estate Entrepreneurship.

- Real Estate Investing typically involves putting money into properties with the expectation of earning returns,

often through a more passive approach. You're primarily focused on earning a return on the money you have invested.
- Real Estate Entrepreneurship, on the other hand, is more hands-on. It involves investing not just money, but also significant time, skills, and effort to create value and generate profits. You're expecting to get a return from the time you're investing and on the money you have invested as well.

So where does flipping properties fit in?

Flipping is primarily an example of Real Estate Entrepreneurship. It requires substantial time and effort in finding deals, managing renovations, and selling properties. You're actively creating value through improvements and leveraging your market knowledge, renovation expertise, and negotiation skills. It's a hands-on business that demands your constant attention and decision-making, making it more entrepreneurial than passive investing.

However, it's worth noting that if you're using a substantial amount of your own cash to fund flips, it can shift the balance somewhat towards investing. But even then, the active nature of flipping keeps it firmly in the entrepreneurial camp. The key is understanding that in flipping, you're not just investing money; you're investing your time and skills to generate returns.

© 2024 James Orr. All rights reserved.

Money Required

Let's break down the money you'll need at various stages of the flipping process:

- **Marketing to Find the Deal** - This is often an overlooked expense, but it's especially important to consider for off-market deals. Often, you'll need funds for marketing to find these potential flip properties. This is especially true if you're looking to utilize creative financing or partner with the seller.
- **Down Payment and Closing Costs** - The amount you'll need varies based on your financing method and flipping strategy. For *Traditional Flipping*, hard money lenders typically require 0-20% down. If you're doing a live-in flip, you might qualify for owner-occupant financing with as little as 0% down (VA/USDA loans), 3% or 5% down (conventional loans), or 3.5% down (FHA loans). *Seller Partnership Flips* with the seller or using a money partner might allow you to flip with no money down since you're relying on the seller's existing financing. Remember, using your own cash instead of financing can improve profitability but ties up more of your capital.
- **Repairs/Rehab Money** - This is often the largest expense in flipping. For *Traditional Flipping*, you might be able to borrow this from your hard money lender. For *Live-in Flips* or *2-Year Tax Advantaged Live-In Flips*, you might need to fund repairs yourself over time or use private lenders to borrow the money. In *Seller Partnership Flips*, these costs might be shared or, more

likely, you will front the money and be reimbursed at sale. Always budget more than you think you'll need for unexpected issues.
- **Holding Costs** - These are ongoing expenses while you own the property. They include loan payments, property taxes, insurance, and utilities. *Traditional Flips* typically have higher holding costs due to higher interest rates on hard money loans. *Live-in Flips* and *2-Year Tax Advantaged Live-In Flips* have lower holding costs as you're living in the property and likely have lower-interest rate, owner-occupant financing. With *Seller Partnership Flips* with the seller, the seller may be paying for holding costs as part of their contribution to the partnership.
- **Marketing/Staging Costs to Sell** - Once your flip is ready, you'll need funds to market it effectively. This might include professional photography, virtual tours, and/or hiring a real estate agent. These costs can often be included in the real estate agent's success fee and paid out of the proceeds of the sale.
- **Reserves for Unexpected Contingencies** - Always set aside extra funds for surprises. This is crucial for all types of flips. Heck, it's crucial for all types of real estate investing. And, out of an abundance of clarity, this is in addition to budgeting more than you're estimating is required for repairs.

Remember, while you can sometimes borrow for expenses like repairs or marketing, it's typically more difficult to borrow for the down payment. Always carefully consider

© 2024 James Orr. All rights reserved.

your financing options and ensure you have adequate funds including reserves before starting your flip.

Credit Required

When it comes to flipping properties, your credit requirements can vary significantly depending on the type of flip you're doing and the financing method you're using.

Here are the main variations:

- **Traditional Flipping** - For *Traditional Flips*, you'll often use hard money loans for the initial purchase. Most hard money lenders will look at your credit score, but their primary focus is often on the property's value and your experience. While it varies, many hard money lenders prefer scores of 620 or higher, though some may work with lower scores if other factors are strong. You may be able to find hard money lenders that don't look at your credit score at all.
- **Live-in Flips** - *Live-In Flips* offer more flexibility in terms of financing options. You can qualify for an FHA loan with a credit score as low as 580, including the FHA 203(k) loan which allows you to finance both the purchase and renovations. If you're a veteran, you might qualify for a VA loan with no set minimum credit score, though many lenders prefer 620 or higher. Conventional loans typically require a minimum score of 620, but higher is preferred for better rates.
- **2-Year Tax-Advantaged Live-In Flips** - The credit requirements for this strategy are like those for *Live-In*

Flips, as you'll be using the same owner-occupant financing.
- **Seller Partnership Flips** - If you're partnering with the seller and using their existing financing, your credit score might not be a factor at all.
- **All-Cash Flips** - If you're fortunate enough to be buying without a loan, no credit score is required. However, keep in mind that a good credit score can still be beneficial for other aspects of your flip, such as obtaining insurance or setting up utility accounts.
- **Credit of Partners** - If you're bringing in a partner for financing (not the seller), their credit score may be more important than yours.

Remember, credit score requirements can change over time and vary by lender. Always check with your local lender for the most up-to-date requirements.

Skills Required

Flipping properties requires a diverse set of skills.

Let's break down the essential abilities you'll need to succeed in this real estate strategy:

- **Finding Deals** - This is the foundation of successful flipping. You'll need to develop a keen eye for undervalued properties and build a stable of reliable sources of deals. This may involve relationships with real estate agents, brokers, and wholesalers as well as marketing to find off-market deals yourself.

- **Rehab Estimating** - Accurately estimating renovation costs is vital to ensure profitability. You'll need to develop a good understanding of construction costs, timelines, and potential issues that may arise during renovations.
- **Acquisition Financing** - Understanding various financing options is key. You'll need to be familiar with traditional mortgages, hard money loans, private lending, and potentially creative financing strategies.
- **Rehab and/or Rehab Management** - This skill involves either doing the renovation work yourself or managing contractors effectively. You'll need to understand construction processes, scheduling, and quality control.
- **Selling Property** - The ability to market and sell your flipped property is crucial. This involves staging, photography, pricing strategy, and negotiation skills. While you can hire a real estate agent, understanding the sales process is beneficial.
- **Exit Financing** - Understanding various financing options for your buyers is also valuable. By knowing how your buyers will be financing your purchase you can avoid doing things that will make their purchase financing harder or impossible.

Many successful flippers start by focusing on one or two key skills and gradually expand their expertise, but this does add to the risk while you lack those skills.

Stability

Shane Parrish, known for his insights on mental models and decision-making through his work at Farnam Street, explores the idea of active versus passive stability in various contexts. This concept applies well to real estate investing, particularly in flipping properties.

Active stability refers to systems or investments that require consistent effort and attention to maintain balance and success, while passive stability involves less frequent intervention.

In real estate, strategies differ in the degree of active stability they demand, but all real estate strategies are active.

- **Traditional Flipping** - This is a prime example of active stability. You're constantly managing multiple moving parts—securing financing, overseeing renovations, and navigating market conditions—all while being mindful of holding costs and timing. It's a high-stakes endeavor that demands continuous attention, rapid decisions, and constant course corrections.
- **Live-In Flips** - These flips also require active stability but tend to be less intense than traditional flipping. Living in the property during renovations gives you more flexibility and time to complete work without the pressure of immediate selling deadlines. Plus, you avoid holding costs on a separate property, easing some of the financial burden while still needing consistent involvement to ensure the project's success.

Scalability

When it comes to scaling your real estate investing, flipping properties presents a unique set of challenges and opportunities.

Let's break down how scalable this strategy is compared to other real estate investing approaches:

- **Deal Flow Limitations** - Finding enough quality deals can be a significant bottleneck in scaling your flipping business. This often results in slower acquisition speed compared to other strategies like buy-and-hold real estate investing.
- **Capital Efficiency** - Flipping can be done with a relatively small amount of capital that's typically reusable after each deal. This recyclable nature of funds allows you to continue and potentially expand your operations over time.
- **Experience Benefits** - The longer you're in the flipping business, the more you'll improve your network, build a reliable team, and enhance your reputation. These factors can contribute to easier scaling as you progress.
- **Time and Labor Intensive** - Flipping requires significant hands-on work, making it challenging to scale as a direct wealth-building strategy. Many investors use profits from flips to acquire more passive assets for long-term wealth growth.
- **Market Dependence** - Your ability to scale can be heavily influenced by local market conditions. In hot

markets, finding deals might be harder, but selling could be easier. The reverse is true in cooler markets.
- **Financing Constraints** - Traditional flipping often relies on hard money loans, which can be more expensive and constricts your ability to scale up.

It's worth noting that different flipping variations can impact scalability:

- **Traditional Flipping** - Offers the most potential for rapid scaling but requires the most active management.
- **Live-in Flips** - Naturally limits your ability to scale quickly as you're living in each property, but can be more manageable for those new to flipping.
- **2-Year Tax Advantaged Live-In Flips** - The slowest to scale due to the extended holding period, but can offer tax benefits that may offset the reduced volume.
- **Seller Partnership Flips** - Can potentially accelerate scaling by leveraging your seller partners' resources, but requires careful management of relationships.

While flipping properties may not be the easiest strategy to scale compared to some passive real estate investments, it can still be a powerful tool in your real estate portfolio, especially when combined with other investing approaches.

And, scaling a flipping business can be done by hiring help which improves your ability to scale significantly.

Risk Exposure

Flipping properties carries a medium risk rating compared to other real estate investing strategies, requiring careful consideration of various factors that can impact your investment.

Here are the key risks you need to be aware of:

- **Renovation Risks** - Unexpected issues during rehabilitation can lead to cost overruns and project delays, potentially eroding your profit margins.
- **Market Volatility** - Interest rate fluctuations during the rehab period may affect buyer financing, potentially impacting your sale price or time-to-sell.
- **Price Decline** - Market shifts during renovation could decrease property value. For longer duration flips like *Live-In Flips* and especially *2-Year Tax Advantaged Live-In Flips*, this extends to a longer-term price decline risk.
- **Financial Exposure** - Your credit score may be impacted if the project doesn't proceed as planned, especially when using leveraged financing.

For partnership flips—with sellers and/or other investors—additional risks include:

- **Reputational Risk** - Unsuccessful partnerships can negatively impact your standing in the real estate community.
- **Partnership Complications** - Misaligned expectations or disagreements with partners can lead to legal and financial challenges.

Each flipping strategy - *Traditional*, *Live-in*, *2-Year Tax Advantaged Live-In*, and *Seller Partnership Flips* - presents a unique risk profile. While *Live-in Flips* may mitigate some

© 2024 James Orr. All rights reserved.

financial risks, they introduce personal challenges of residing in an active construction zone.

Proper risk management, thorough due diligence, and a comprehensive understanding of market dynamics are crucial for navigating these challenges and maximizing the potential returns of property flipping.

Profit Speed

Let's break down the returns you can expect while flipping properties and how quickly you might see that profit.

First, let's talk about the four primary returns in real estate investing:

- **Appreciation** - With flipping, you're mainly focused on forced appreciation through renovations, but you might catch some organic appreciation too, especially with longer duration flips like the two variations of live-in flips.

- **Cash Flow** - Unless you're renting out the property (which is rare in flipping), you won't typically see traditional cash flow.
- **Debt Paydown** - If you're using interest-only loans (common in flipping), you won't benefit from debt paydown. However, the two variations of live-in flips with amortizing loans can offer this benefit.
- **Tax Benefits** - Flippers typically can't take advantage of depreciation benefits like *Cash Flow from Depreciation*™, as they're not renting the property.

There's also a secondary return to consider: the interest you earn on your reserves set aside for unexpected costs.

Now, let's talk profit speed and size:

- **Speed of Profit** - You can typically see profits within 6 months after purchasing the property. You need enough time to purchase, rehab, and sell the property. It's often a much faster turnaround compared to buy-and-hold strategies.
- **Profit Size** - Many flippers aim for a fixed dollar amount, often between $10,000 to $30,000 per flip net after all expenses (except taxes). Others target a percentage of the property value, usually 10-15%. There is a lot of variation in profit size and some flippers insist on much larger profit spreads. Some flippers will take skinnier deals to keep their team of contractors working so they don't disappear for more profitable deals. Others choose as their strategy to do fewer, but more profitable deals.

Remember, if you're doing *Seller Partnership Flips*, you'll be sharing these profits with the seller based on your agreement.

While flipping can offer quick profits, it's important to note that you're trading time for money. It's more of a job than a passive investment, but for many, the potential for larger, faster returns makes it an attractive strategy.

Finding Deals

Let's discuss how you might find properties to flip.

There are some common methods and some more unusual, less common methods.

Most Common Methods

Here are the most common methods for finding properties to flip:

- **Multiple Listing Service (MLS)** - This is your go-to resource for finding potential flip properties. It's a comprehensive database of properties listed by real estate agents. You'll find a wide variety of options here, including some that might be perfect for flipping.
- **For Sale By Owner (FSBO)** - These are properties where the owner is directly selling without an agent. They come in two main varieties:
    - **Actively Marketed** - These properties are openly advertised by the owners. You might find them on

websites, social media, or with "For Sale" signs in the yard. They can be great opportunities if you're quick and persuasive.
- **Hidden** - These are potential opportunities that aren't actively on the market. To uncover these flip opportunities, you'll need to be proactive through marketing and/or networking.
    - **Marketing** - Create targeted campaigns to reach potential sellers. This could include direct mail, online ads, or even door-knocking in areas you're interested in. For example, direct mail marketing into neighborhoods that are seeing higher than normal flips could be a great way to uncover additional flip opportunities.
    - **Networking** - Build relationships in your target areas. Attend local events, join community groups, and let people know you're in the market to buy properties. You never know who might be considering selling their home.

- **Wholesalers** - These are individuals or companies that find off-market properties and sell them to investors like you. They often have access to deeply discounted properties that could be perfect for flipping. Building relationships with reputable wholesalers in your area can give you access to deals you might not find elsewhere.

Remember, diversifying your deal-finding strategies is key. The perfect flip opportunity might come from any of these sources, so cast a wide net.

More Unusual Methods

While the Multiple Listing Service (MLS) and For Sale By Owner (FSBO) properties are the most common sources for finding flip opportunities, there are some less conventional methods that savvy investors use to uncover potential deals.

Let's explore these less common, more unusual, alternative approaches:

- **Auctions** - Property auctions can be a great additional source for finding discounted properties. These include foreclosure auctions, estate sales, and government auctions. Keep in mind that properties are often sold "as-is," so thorough due diligence is crucial before bidding.
- **Foreclosures and IRS Seizures** - Properties in foreclosure or seized by the IRS can often be purchased at a discount. You can find these listings through county records, specialized websites, or by working with banks directly. Be prepared for potential competition and slightly more complex purchasing processes.
- **Real Estate Owned (REOs)** - These are properties that have been foreclosed on and are now owned by the bank. REOs can be great opportunities as banks are often motivated to sell quickly. You can find REO listings on bank websites, through REO specialists, or on the Multiple Listing Services once the bank has opted to list them for sale.
- **Tax Lien and Tax Deed Sales** - When property owners fail to pay their property taxes, local governments may

auction off tax liens or the properties themselves. This can be a way to acquire properties for back taxes owed, which is often significantly less than market value. However, these sales can be complex, highly competitive and may require a waiting period before you can take possession of the property.

Remember, while these methods can lead to great deals, they often require more research, due diligence, and sometimes specialized knowledge of legal processes. It's always a good idea to consult with a real estate attorney or experienced local expert when venturing into these less common methods of property acquisition.

Searching for Fixer Upper Deals

When searching for properties to flip inside the Multiple Listing Service (MLS), you'll want to use some smart strategies to uncover those flip opportunities.

Here are some tips to help you find the perfect fixer-upper:

- **Use "Fixer-Upper" Keywords** - Search for terms like "handyman special," "fixer," "TLC," "needs work," or "as-is" in the property descriptions. These can often indicate properties with potential for renovation and profit.
- **Look for Problem Indicators** - Include keywords such as "mold," "asbestos," "damage," "fire," "smoke," or "water damage" in your searches. While these issues

can be serious, they often scare away less experienced buyers, potentially leaving opportunities for you.
- **Leverage the Tax-to-List Price Ratio** - Use property taxes as a proxy for value. A high tax-to-list price ratio might indicate a property that's undervalued. Set up custom searches to flag these potential deals or export a list of properties for sale to a spreadsheet and sort by this ratio.
- **Focus on Long-Standing Listings** - Properties that have been on the market for an extended period might have motivated sellers. Look for listings that are 60 days or older.
- **Set Up Automated Searches** - Create saved searches with your specific criteria in the MLS. This way, you'll be notified as soon as a potential flip hits the market.
- **Look for Estate Sales** - These properties often need updates and may be priced to sell quickly. Search for terms like "estate sale" or "probate" in the listing descriptions.
- **Consider Foreclosures and Bank-Owned Properties** - While these can be competitive, they often present good opportunities for flips. Look for "REO" (Real Estate Owned) or "foreclosure" in the listing details.

Remember, the key to finding great flip opportunities in the MLS is to be creative with your searches and persistent in your efforts.

Ask your preferred real estate agent to set up automatic searches with all these terms to be sent to you as soon as they hit the market. Then, you'll need to be looking at those emails and moving quickly if any look even remotely promising.

Analyzing Deals

When it comes to analyzing properties for flipping, you'll need a specialized tool tailored for this unique investment strategy. While *The World's Greatest Real Estate Deal Analysis Spreadsheet*™ is excellent for rental properties, it's not designed for flips.

Instead, you'll want to use a spreadsheet specifically created for flipping properties. This tool should allow you to input crucial data points such as:

- **Purchase Price** - The amount you'll pay for the property, including any closing costs.
- **Renovation Costs** - A detailed breakdown of all repairs and upgrades you plan to make.
- **Holding Costs** - Expenses like property taxes, insurance, and utilities during the renovation period.
- **After Repair Value (ARV)** - The estimated selling price of the property after renovations.
- **Selling Costs** - Real estate agent commissions, closing costs, and any other fees associated with selling the property.

A good flipping analysis spreadsheet will use these inputs to calculate your potential profit, return on investment, and other key metrics specific to flipping. This will help you make informed decisions about which properties are worth pursuing.

© 2024 James Orr. All rights reserved.

Remember, accurate analysis is crucial in flipping.

Even small miscalculations can significantly impact your profits.

Take the time to research and input realistic numbers into your spreadsheet for the best results.

Market Conditions

What are the best markets to flip properties? What are the markets that will prove to be the most challenging when flipping properties?

Ideal

These are the most ideal market conditions for flipping properties:

- **Markets Where You Can Buy Properties That Need Work at a Discount** - Look for areas with a high number of distressed or foreclosed properties. These markets often offer opportunities to purchase homes below market value, giving you more room for profit after renovations.
- **Value Add Opportunities** - Seek out neighborhoods where small improvements can lead to significant increases in property value. This might include up-and-coming areas or those undergoing revitalization, where your renovations can have a big impact on the final sale price.

© 2024 James Orr. All rights reserved.

- **Markets with Strong Demand** - Focus on areas with a robust real estate market and high buyer interest. Strong demand ensures that your renovated property will sell quickly, reducing holding costs and increasing your overall profit.

Challenging

While flipping properties can be lucrative, certain market conditions can make it challenging. One of the most difficult scenarios you might encounter is:

- **Few Opportunities** - Seems obvious, but markets where there are not many flip opportunities are challenging to fix and flip in.
- **Low Buyer Demand** - In a market with few interested buyers, your beautifully renovated property might sit unsold for longer than anticipated. This can lead to increased holding costs, eating into your potential profits. You might find yourself in a situation where you need to lower your asking price to attract buyers, potentially reducing your return on investment.

Accessibility/Availability

When it comes to finding properties to flip, accessibility and availability can vary greatly depending on your market and strategy.

Here are some key points to consider:

- **Scarcity of Deals** - Finding flip-worthy properties can be challenging. You're looking for homes that are undervalued and have potential for significant value increase after renovations.
- **Easier than BRRRR** - While still difficult, locating flip properties is generally easier than finding BRRRR deals. This is because you don't need to factor in long-term cash flow potential like you do when acquiring BRRRR properties. You only need to find properties that you can buy, add value and resell for a profit. With BRRRR you need to buy, add value, put a tenant in the property and get profitable income on it and then be able to refi the property.
- **Market Saturation Warning** - Be cautious in markets with high availability of potential flip properties. This could indicate a slower selling market, which might extend your holding time and eat into profits.
- **Market Variations** - Some real estate markets are more conducive to flipping than others. Look for areas with a good balance of distressed properties and strong buyer demand.
- **Remote Market Potential** - If your local market is tough, consider investing in remote markets. This can open up more opportunities but comes with its own set of challenges, such as managing renovations from afar.

Remember, the key to successful flipping is finding the right balance between property availability and market demand.

It's a skill that often improves with experience and thorough market research.

© 2024 James Orr. All rights reserved.

Using Retirement Account

Self-directed retirement accounts offer powerful opportunities for real estate investing, including property flips. However, it's important to know the rules. Financing can be tricky, often requiring larger down payments and variable interest rates.

IRS regulations prohibit self-dealing, which means you can't personally work on properties owned by your retirement account. You'll need to hire third-party contractors for any renovations.

Using your retirement funds as a money partner in someone else's flip can help you avoid some complexities. Since properties held in retirement accounts can't be used for personal purposes, both variations of live-in flips are off-limits with these funds.

- **Borrow From SD401k** - You can borrow from your Self-Directed 401k (SD401k) for a down payment or repair costs. Borrowing allows you to invest in the property and still comply with IRS rules, but you'll need to repay the loan, typically within five years.
- **Use SD401k Funds for Repairs** - Instead of using retirement funds for the whole project, consider using them just for repairs. This gives you more flexibility, especially when doing live-in flips, while maintaining liquidity for other investments.

1 Rental = 1 Flip/Year

Recent modeling using the *Real Estate Financial Planner*™ (REFP) software compared rental properties and flips.

The analysis shows that annual returns from one rental property can often match those from a single flip.

However, the strategies are very different. Flipping is active and time-intensive, often requiring a full-time commitment.

Owning rental properties, especially with professional management, can be more passive.

For example, imagine owning 10 rental properties. The annual returns could be like doing 10 flips in a year.

The big difference? Managing 10 rentals with help from property managers requires much less day-to-day involvement than completing 10 flips.

This shows how rental properties can be a more efficient, long-term wealth-building strategy.

© 2024 James Orr. All rights reserved.

You not only gain ongoing returns but also build a system for generating passive income over time.

Keep in mind, real estate markets vary. Returns depend on property values, rental rates, and local conditions.

Always do thorough, market-specific analysis using tools like the REFP software before making decisions.

BONUS CHAPTERS

© 2024 James Orr. All rights reserved.

Introduction to Real Estate Deal Analysis

Analyzing real estate deals can be a daunting task, but with the right tools and knowledge, it becomes much more manageable. One powerful tool we recommend is *The World's Greatest Real Estate Deal Analysis Spreadsheet*™. This spreadsheet is designed to help you evaluate the financial viability of real estate investments with ease and precision.

In our book, *How to Analyze Real Estate Deals*, we delve deep into the intricacies of deal analysis, providing step-by-step instructions and expert insights. This introduction aims to give you a high-level overview of the process and how to effectively use the spreadsheet to make informed investment decisions.

© 2024 James Orr. All rights reserved.

The spreadsheet allows you to input various data points such as purchase price, mortgage details, monthly income, and annual expenses. It then performs complex calculations to provide you with key metrics like cash flow, return on investment (ROI), and internal rate of return (IRR).

By leveraging this tool, you can:

- Quickly assess the profitability of potential deals.
- Compare multiple investment opportunities.
- Make data-driven decisions to maximize your returns.

Whether you're a seasoned investor or just starting out, understanding how to analyze real estate deals is crucial for success.

Download Spreadsheet for Free

© 2024 James Orr. All rights reserved.

Unlock the full potential of your real estate investments by downloading *The World's Greatest Real Estate Deal Analysis Spreadsheet*™ for free.

Get your copy at: https://REFP.info/spreadsheet

We recommend always keeping an unedited, fresh copy on your hard drive in case you can't download the spreadsheet in the future.

Before analyzing a property, always make a new copy.

Spreadsheet Inputs

Entering the inputs into the spreadsheet is simple. Here's what you need to know:

- The manila fields indicate where you should input your data.
- The gray background with blue text shows the calculations that are automatically performed for you.

First, please name the deal that you're analyzing in the field just above the "Purchase Inputs". This will allow you to know which deal you're looking at if you're considering analyzing multiple deals or one deal multiple ways.

Purchase Inputs

Before we dive into the specifics of analyzing a real estate deal, let's go over the inputs required for the spreadsheet. These inputs will be divided into two columns: one for percentages and one for dollar amounts (or numbers).

Understanding what to enter in each field is crucial for accurately analyzing your deal. Let's go over what to put in each field next.

- **ARV** - Enter the After Repair Value, which is the estimated value of the property after all repairs and improvements have been made.
- **Purchase Price** - Enter the amount you are paying to acquire the property from the seller.
- **Seller Concessions** - Enter any financial concessions or incentives that the seller has agreed to provide, such as covering closing costs or offering repair credits.
- **Down Payment** - Enter the initial amount you will pay out-of-pocket towards the purchase of the property. Be sure to check out our guide on creative ways to come up with down payments for rental properties.
- **Closing Costs** - Enter the total costs associated with closing the real estate transaction, including title insurance, attorney fees, and other related expenses.
- **Rent Ready Costs** - Enter the expenses required to make the property ready for tenants, such as cleaning, repairs, and any necessary upgrades.
- **Cumulative Negative Cash Flow** - If you have negative cash flow enter the total cumulative amount of negative cash flow you anticipate before the property becomes cash flow positive. We recommend you set this aside to reduce risk. You may also want to check out our book on *How to Improve Cash Flow on Rental Properties* to get rid of negative cash flow on your properties.
- **Total Invested** - This is calculated for you. It is the cumulative amount of money you have invested in the

© 2024 James Orr. All rights reserved.

property, including **Down Payment**, **Closing Costs**, **Rent Ready Costs**, **Cumulative Negative Cash Flow**, minus any **Seller Concessions** you received from the seller.

Mortgage Inputs

To accurately analyze your real estate deal, it's essential to input detailed information about your mortgage and financing. These inputs will help calculate your monthly payments, interest costs, and overall financial commitment. Here's what you'll need to enter:

- **Mortgage Amount** - This is calculated for you. It is the total amount of money you are borrowing to finance the purchase of the property.
- **Mortgage Interest Rate** - Enter the annual interest rate for your mortgage. This is the percentage of the loan amount that you will pay as interest each year.
- **Loan Term** - Enter the duration of your mortgage loan in months. 360 months is a 30-year loan. This is the period over which you will repay the loan.
- **Private Mortgage Insurance** - Enter the monthly cost of private mortgage insurance (PMI) if applicable. PMI is typically required if your down payment is less than 20% of the purchase price. If you don't have PMI, use 0.000% here.
- **Drop PMI LTV** - Enter the loan-to-value (LTV) ratio at which PMI will be dropped. This is the point at which your equity in the property is high enough that PMI is no

longer required. If you don't have PMI, use 0.000% here.

Monthly Income

Accurately estimating your monthly income is critical for assessing the profitability of your real estate investment. This section will guide you through the necessary inputs for calculating your expected monthly income from the property, including rent and any additional sources of income.

- **Monthly Rent** - Enter the amount of rent you expect to receive from tenants each month. If you don't know how to determine what rent is on a property you're considering, you might want to check out our book on *How to Determine Rent Comps*.
- **Monthly Other Income** - Enter any additional monthly income from the property, such as parking fees, laundry services, or storage rentals.

Annual Expenses

Understanding and accurately estimating annual expenses is crucial for analyzing the financial viability of a real estate investment. This section will guide you through the various costs associated with owning and maintaining a property, from vacancy rates to property taxes and insurance. By thoroughly accounting for each of these expenses, you can better predict your investment's profitability and make more informed decisions.

- **Vacancy Rate** - Enter the percentage of time the property is expected to be vacant each year.
- **Property Taxes** - Enter the annual property tax amount you will pay for owning the property.
- **Property Insurance** - Enter the annual cost of insuring the property.
- **HOA Dues** - Enter the annual homeowner association fees, if applicable.
- **Utilities** - Enter the annual cost of utilities that you will pay as the property owner.
- **Other Expenses 1 and 2** - Enter any other annual expenses not covered in the previous categories.
- **Maintenance** - Enter the annual cost of maintaining the property, including repairs and routine upkeep.
- **CapEx** - Enter the annual amount set aside for capital expenditures. Consider our book and spreadsheet on CapEx for more guidance.
- **Management** - Enter the annual cost of property management services, if applicable.

Depreciation Details

Depreciation is a critical aspect of real estate investment analysis, as it allows you to account for the gradual reduction in the value of your property over time. Properly calculating and understanding depreciation can provide significant tax benefits and improve the overall financial picture of your investment. This section will guide you through the necessary inputs for determining depreciation, including land value, property type, and your effective income tax rate. By accurately inputting these details, you can optimize your investment strategy and maximize potential returns.

- **Land Value** - Enter the percent of the property that represents the value of the land. This value is used to calculate depreciation.
- **Property Type (C or R)** - Indicate whether the property is classified as commercial (C) or residential (R). This affects the depreciation schedule.
- **Effective Income Tax Rate** - Enter your effective income tax rate. This rate is used to estimate the tax benefits of depreciation.

Overrides

The spreadsheet is designed to be user-friendly on the Dashboard, while offering extensive functionality in the Overrides section. This dual approach ensures that users can easily navigate and input basic data, but also have access to more advanced features when needed.

In the Overrides tab, you have the ability to:

- **Modify any other inputs** - Adjust various parameters to suit your specific needs and scenarios.
- **Perform custom calculations** - Create and implement your own unique calculations to gain deeper insights into your investments.

© 2024 James Orr. All rights reserved.

- **View intermediate calculations** - Access detailed breakdowns of the calculations that drive the final results, providing transparency and better understanding.
- **Analyze performance over an extended period** - The spreadsheet allows you to conduct analysis through up to 40 years, enabling long-term strategic planning.
- **Track investment performance** - Use the Overrides tab to monitor how your investment evolves over time, making it easier to adjust your strategy as needed.

This comprehensive functionality ensures that the spreadsheet is not only a powerful tool for initial analysis but also a valuable resource for ongoing management and optimization of your real estate investments.

Dashboard

The Dashboard section provides a comprehensive overview of your real estate investment's key metrics and financial performance.

Here, you can quickly assess your monthly cash flow, return on investment (ROI), internal rate of return (IRR), and other critical indicators.

The Dashboard is designed to offer a user-friendly summary of your investment, allowing you to make informed decisions and track your progress over time.

Of course, you can dig into the Overrides tab for a ridiculous amount of additional detail.

Monthly Cash Flow - Year 1

This chart displays the Monthly Cash Flow, *Cash Flow from Depreciation*™, and the combined total, referred to as *True Cash Flow*™.

Understanding these metrics is crucial as they provide a comprehensive view of your investment's financial health.

- Monthly Cash Flow shows the actual cash inflow and outflow.
- *Cash Flow from Depreciation*™ accounts for tax benefits derived from property depreciation.
- *True Cash Flow*™ combines these figures, offering a more accurate representation of your investment's profitability.

Return in Dollars - Year 1

This chart displays the estimated dollars earned from your real estate investment over the first year, including Appreciation, Cash Flow, *Cash Flow from Depreciation*™, and Debt Paydown.

Understanding these metrics provides a holistic view of your investment's performance:

- **Appreciation** - Reflects the increase in property value over the year.
- **Cash Flow** - Shows the actual cash inflow and outflow.
- **Cash Flow from Depreciation**™ - Accounts for tax benefits derived from property depreciation.

© 2024 James Orr. All rights reserved.

- **Debt Paydown** - Indicates the amount of principal paid down on your mortgage over the year.

Additionally, the chart includes earnings on reserves:

- **6 Months of Reserves in Savings** - Illustrates the interest earned if you set aside 6 months of reserves in a savings account.
- **Most of 12 Months of Reserves in Another Investment** - Shows the potential earnings if most of 12 months of reserves are invested in another investment vehicle like the stock market.

These combined figures provide a comprehensive representation of your investment's profitability and financial health over the first year.

You can see the totals at the bottom of the chart.

Return on Investment - Year 1

This chart displays the return on investment (ROI) from your real estate investment over the first year, including Appreciation, Cash Flow, *Cash Flow from Depreciation*™, and Debt Paydown.

Understanding these metrics provides a holistic view of your investment's performance:

- **Appreciation** - Reflects the increase in property value over the year divided by the total amount invested (and reserves where applicable).

- **Cash Flow** - Shows the actual cash inflow and outflow divided by the total amount invested (and reserves where applicable).
- **Cash Flow from Depreciation**™ - Accounts for tax benefits derived from property depreciation divided by the total amount invested (and reserves where applicable).
- **Debt Paydown** - Indicates the amount of principal paid down on your mortgage over the year divided by the total amount invested (and reserves where applicable).

Additionally, the chart includes ROI on reserves:

- **6 Months of Reserves in Savings** - Illustrates the interest earned if you set aside 6 months of reserves in a savings account, divided by the total amount invested plus 6 months of reserves.
- **Most of 12 Months of Reserves in Another Investment** - Shows the potential earnings if most of 12 months of reserves are invested in another investment vehicle like the stock market, divided by the total amount invested plus 12 months of reserves.

These combined figures provide a comprehensive representation of your investment's profitability and financial health over the first year in terms of ROI.

You can see the totals at the bottom of the chart.

© 2024 James Orr. All rights reserved.

Returns if Sold (ROI and IRR)

This chart illustrates the return on investment if you sold the property each year for the first 20 years. It includes three key metrics:

- **Simple Annualized Return on Investment** - This metric shows the average annual return on your investment, calculated by dividing the total return by the number of years you held the property.
- **Compound Annualized Return on Investment** - This metric accounts for the compounding effect, showing the average annual return on your investment when considering the reinvestment of earnings.
- **Internal Rate of Return (IRR)** - This metric represents the annualized rate of return that makes the net present value (NPV) of all cash flows (both inflows and outflows) from the investment equal to zero.

These metrics provide a comprehensive view of the financial performance of your investment over time, helping you to understand the potential long-term profitability and compare it with other investment opportunities.

Cash on Cash ROI & Cap Rate - Years 1-5

This chart displays the Cash on Cash Return on Investment (ROI) and the Capitalization Rate (Cap Rate) for the property over the first 5 years.

Understanding these metrics provides a comprehensive view of your investment's performance:

- **Cash on Cash ROI** - This metric shows the annual return on your investment based on the actual cash invested. It is calculated by dividing the annual pre-tax cash flow by the total cash invested.
- **Cap Rate** - This metric represents the annual return on the property based on its current market value. It is calculated by dividing the net operating income (NOI) by the property's current market value.

By understanding these metrics, you can gauge the effectiveness and profitability of your investment, enabling you to make well-informed decisions and evaluate it against other potential investment opportunities.

Return on True Net Equity™

This chart shows you the returns you're earning from Appreciation, Cash Flow, *Cash Flow from Depreciation*™, and Debt Paydown divided by the equity minus the costs to access that equity with a sale (what we call True Net Equity™). It shows the first 20 years. It also shows the total of all four areas of return.

Understanding these metrics is crucial for assessing the true profitability of your real estate investment:

- **Appreciation** - Reflects the increase in property value over the year.
- **Cash Flow** - Shows the actual cash inflow and outflow.

© 2024 James Orr. All rights reserved.

- **Cash Flow from Depreciation**™ - Accounts for tax benefits derived from property depreciation.
- **Debt Paydown** - Indicates the amount of principal paid down on your mortgage over the year.

By dividing these returns by the True Net Equity™, you get a more accurate representation of your investment's performance, considering the costs to access the equity. This comprehensive view helps in making informed decisions and comparing the potential returns of different investments.

For more information on True Net Equity™ consider checking out our books about that:

- Should I Sell My Rental My Rental Property?
- Should I Sell My Refinance My Rental Property?

Annual Key Metrics - Year 1

This chart displays the financial performance of your real estate investment in terms of Gross Potential Income (GPI), Gross Operating Income (GOI), Operating Expenses (OpEx), and Net Operating Income (NOI) for the first year.

Understanding these metrics provides a comprehensive view of your investment's revenue and profitability:

- **Gross Potential Income (GPI)** - This metric represents the total income the property could generate if it were fully rented and all units were occupied at market rent rates, without accounting for any vacancies or losses.

- **Gross Operating Income (GOI)** - This metric reflects the actual income received from the property, including rent and other income sources, after accounting for vacancies and any collection losses.
- **Operating Expenses (OpEx)** - These are the costs associated with maintaining and managing the property, excluding mortgage payments and capital expenditures.
- **Net Operating Income (NOI)** - This metric is calculated by subtracting the operating expenses from the Gross Operating Income. It represents the income generated by the property after all operating expenses have been deducted.

By understanding these metrics, you can better assess the financial health and profitability of your real estate investment, helping you make more strategic decisions and compare it with other investment opportunities.

Annual Non-Loan Expenses - Year 1

This chart displays the financial performance of your real estate investment by itemizing all the non-loan expenses for the first year. Understanding these metrics provides a comprehensive view of your property's operational costs, which are crucial for accurate financial analysis and planning:

- **Vacancy Rate** - The percentage of time the property is expected to be vacant each year.
- **Property Taxes** - The annual amount paid for property taxes.

- **Property Insurance** - The cost of insuring the property for the year.
- **HOA Dues** - Annual homeowner association fees, if applicable.
- **Utilities** - The total annual cost of utilities paid by the property owner.
- **Other Expenses 1 and 2** - Any additional annual expenses not covered in the previous categories.
- **Maintenance** - The annual expense for maintaining the property, including routine repairs and upkeep.
- **CapEx** - The annual amount set aside for capital expenditures, such as major repairs or replacements.
- **Management Fees** - The cost of property management services, if utilized.

By breaking down these non-loan expenses, this chart helps you understand the total operational costs associated with your property, enabling you to better manage your investment and forecast its financial performance.

Equities and Cost-To-Access

This chart displays the equity in your real estate deal each year for the first 20 years, focusing on two key metrics: *True Net Equity*™ and Cash-Out Refi Equity.

- ***True Net Equity*™** - This is the equity minus the costs to access it through a sale. It shows the real profit after considering selling costs.

© 2024 James Orr. All rights reserved.

- **Cash-Out Refi Equity** - This is the equity available if you refinance the property. It helps you understand the potential funds available through refinancing.
- **Cost-To-Access Equity Percentages** - The chart also shows the costs (as a percentage of the equity) associated with accessing each type of equity. This provides insight into the expenses involved.

Understanding these metrics is crucial for knowing how much money you could pull out of the investment over time and the cost to access that equity if you choose to do so.

Trademarks: The World's Greatest Real Estate Deal Analysis Spreadsheet™, Cash Flow from Depreciation™, True Cash Flow, True Net Equity™, and Nomad™ are trademarks of James Orr and/or Real Estate Financial Planner LLC. All rights reserved.

© 2024 James Orr. All rights reserved.

94 Ways to Improve Cash Flow on Rental Properties

You might find yourself in a real estate market where:

- Property prices are high—possibly even soaring,
- Mortgage interest rates are elevated—maybe significantly so,
- Yet rents, despite any increases, haven't risen enough to offset these higher prices and rates.

Instead of the steady stream of cash flow you anticipated, you may be seeing just a trickle.

As a real estate broker, I developed the *Lowest Monthly Payment Guarantee*™ for my clients. This comprehensive checklist—backed by a *cash-in-your-pocket guarantee*—promised to uncover every possible way to reduce and minimize their monthly payments when purchasing a property.

© 2024 James Orr. All rights reserved.

For my real estate investor clients, I went a step further and created the *Maximum Cash Flow Guarantee*™. This second checklist—also backed by a *cash-in-your-pocket guarantee*—was designed to help them identify every possible way to increase and maximize the income generated from their rental properties.

Simply put, cash flow is the difference between income and expenses.

By maximizing income and minimizing expenses on a rental property, you can significantly boost your cash flow.

Below, you'll find an abridged version of these two checklists—combined into one—designed to help you maximize cash flow on your rental properties.

For your convenience, I've organized the strategies into seven distinct stages of the real estate investing process.

7 Distinct Real Estate Investing Stages for Improving Cash Flow

The real estate investing process can be broken down into seven distinct stages, each offering unique opportunities to improve cash flow:

1. **Searching for Properties** - Strategies to enhance cash flow while you're searching for a property to buy.

2. **Financing the Property** - Tactics to maximize cash flow when securing financing for the property you're purchasing.
3. **Improving the Real Estate Investing Strategy** - Different real estate investing strategies produce varying levels of cash flow. Here, you'll find strategies tailored to the specific investing approach you choose once you've acquired the property.
4. **Improving the Property** - Cash flow enhancement strategies based on making physical improvements to the property itself.
5. **Marketing the Property for Rent** - Techniques to boost cash flow during the process of marketing your property to prospective tenants.
6. **While Owning the Property** - Strategies you can implement at any time during ownership to optimize cash flow.
7. **While Renting the Property** - Methods to improve cash flow while actively renting out the property.

While applying strategies from each stage will maximize your cash flow, you can also focus on the stage you're currently in. Implement what you can now, and revisit these strategies regularly to continuously improve—aim for just a 1% improvement each month.

Searching for Properties

Here are the cash flow improving strategies to implement while searching for a property to buy.

© 2024 James Orr. All rights reserved.

- **Agent Selection** - Choosing the right real estate agent can have a significant impact on your investment's cash flow. Some agents offer lower commissions or commission rebates. This money can appear as improved cash flow in the first year or use the money to buy down your mortgage interest rate and get improved cash flow for the life of the loan.
- **Lock/Float** - When securing financing for a property, interest rates can fluctuate. Locking in an interest rate early can protect you from rising rates during the closing process, while floating allows you to benefit from potential rate drops. This decision can directly influence your cash flow by affecting your monthly mortgage payments. This is especially important when buying properties that have extended under contract periods like when buying new construction.
- **Search for Less Expensive Properties** - Lower-priced properties often come with smaller mortgage payments, which can improve cash flow if you're able to get the same rent as their more expensive alternatives. For every $10,000 less expensive the property, you save approximately $50 per month (when mortgage rates are in the 5% range). Some lower priced prices will have commensurately lower rents. Analyze each deal carefully to ensure that the overall income and expenses align to boost your cash flow.
- **Search for Pretty Properties** - Consider purchasing properties that are already in good condition and don't require significant fix-up costs. By doing so, you can allocate funds that would have been used for repairs to

increase your down payment or buy down the interest rate, both of which can lead to better cash flow.
- **Search for Seller Concessions** - Seller concessions are contributions from the seller to help cover your closing costs. By negotiating for these concessions, you can reduce your out-of-pocket expenses or even use them to buy down your mortgage interest rate, both of which enhance cash flow. Consider searching for properties that are offering seller concessions.
- **Search for Creative Financing** - Creative financing can offer more favorable terms than traditional loans, directly impacting your cash flow. Here are several types of creative financing to consider:
    - **Search for Owner Financing** - Owner financing involves the seller acting as the lender, which can lead to better terms than a traditional bank loan. This can reduce your monthly payments and improve cash flow. We define owner financing as when the seller does not have a mortgage; if they have a mortgage that's wrap financing or buying the property subject to their existing mortgage which we will cover next.
    - **Search for Wrap Financing** - In wrap financing, you agree to pay the seller a monthly amount that "wraps" around their existing mortgage. The seller keeps their original mortgage in place and continues making payments to their lender. You, in turn, make payments to the seller that cover both the existing mortgage and any additional amount you've agreed upon. This can result in a lower overall interest rate compared to obtaining new financing, which can

improve your cash flow. Wrap financing also gives the seller the protection of foreclosure rights if you fail to make payments.

- **Search for Subject To**- In a "subject to" arrangement, you take ownership of the property while the seller's original mortgage stays in place. Instead of wrapping a new loan around the old one, you take over making payments directly to the lender on the seller's existing loan. The loan remains in the seller's name, but you're responsible for the payments. You're not formally accountable to the lender—it's not on your credit report—but you are responsible to the seller as per your agreement. This can be advantageous if the seller's mortgage has a lower interest rate than what's currently available. Like wrap financing, this can significantly reduce your mortgage expenses and boost cash flow. However, "subject to" financing typically doesn't offer the seller the same foreclosure protections as wrap financing does.
- **Search for Assumable Loans** - Some loans can be formally transferred from the seller to the buyer, keeping the original interest rate intact. If the seller's loan has a lower interest rate, assuming the loan can significantly boost your cash flow. Since most loan assumptions are for owner-occupant borrowers this strategy likely only applies to those utilizing an owner-occupant investing strategy like house hacking or Nomad™.
- **Search for Rent-To-Own Properties** - Rent-to-own agreements allow you to lease a property with the

© 2024 James Orr. All rights reserved.

option to purchase it later. These arrangements can offer lower initial payments and more flexible terms, which may improve your cash flow compared to traditional financing.
- **Search for Agreements for Deed** - Also called bond for deed, contract for deed, or installment land contracts, these arrangements let you pay the seller directly over time. You get the deed after fulfilling the contract. This can lead to lower payments and improved cash flow while you're repaying.
- **Search for Seller Financing** - Seller financing typically involves the seller offering a loan to cover a portion of the purchase price, often as a second mortgage or "carryback" loan. In this scenario, you would secure the primary mortgage from a traditional lender, and the seller finances the remaining balance. For example, if you purchase a property for $200,000, you might get a $160,000 loan from a bank, with the seller providing a $40,000 loan. This setup can result in more favorable terms, such as lower interest rates or flexible payment schedules, improving your overall cash flow. Unlike owner financing, where the seller finances the entire purchase, seller financing usually complements other financing sources, reducing the need for a larger bank loan.

Once you've found a promising property using the strategies above, the next step is to optimize your financing to further enhance your cash flow. Let's explore the various ways you can improve your cash flow during the financing stage of your real estate investment.

Financing the Property

Here are the cash flow improving strategies to implement while financing the property you're buying.

Before Getting Loan

Here are a few strategies to improve cash flow to use before getting your loan.

- **Lender Selection** - Shop around for lenders to find one that offers better interest rates, lower fees, or more favorable terms. Different lenders have varying costs and requirements, so comparing multiple options on the same day can ensure you get the best deal, improving your overall cash flow.
- **Select by Closing Costs** - Some loans come with higher closing costs than others. By selecting a loan with lower closing costs, especially if you plan to finance these costs, you can reduce the amount you need to borrow, leading to better cash flow due to lower monthly payments.
- **Lock/Float** - Decide whether to lock in your interest rate early to protect against potential rate increases before closing, or to float and take advantage of possible rate decreases. Locking your rate provides security, while floating offers flexibility, both of which can impact your cash flow depending on market conditions.

- **Offer Less** - Negotiating a lower purchase price directly reduces the amount you need to finance, leading to lower monthly mortgage payments. This strategy can also leave more of your resources available for other cash flow improvement tactics.

Pay Upfront Instead of Financing

Here are some strategies for improving cash flow that deal with opting to pay fees upfront instead of financing them.

- **Seller Concessions** - Negotiate for the seller to cover some of your closing costs or to provide credits that can be used to buy down your mortgage interest rate. This is almost certainly required to be done at the time you make your offer and not after your offer is accepted. This reduces your upfront cash outlay and can lower your monthly mortgage payments, thereby improving cash flow.
- **Pay Closing Costs** - Paying your closing costs upfront instead of rolling them into your mortgage can reduce the amount you borrow, lowering your monthly payments and improving cash flow over the life of the loan.
- **Pre-Pay PMI** - If you're required to pay Private Mortgage Insurance (PMI), consider pre-paying it in a lump sum rather than monthly. This reduces your ongoing monthly expenses, leading to better cash flow.
- **Staggered Rate** - Opt for a staggered interest rate loan, where the interest rate is lower in the initial years

and increases over time. This can provide you with better cash flow during the early years of the loan when you may need it most.
- **Buy Down Rate** - Pay upfront to lower your mortgage interest rate for the life of the loan. A lower interest rate means a lower monthly payment, which can significantly improve your cash flow over time. For long-term buy and hold real estate investors—especially if you find yourself in a low mortgage interest rate environment—this can be an amazing strategy.

Change/Improve Borrower(s)

These strategies for improving cash flow relate to changing or improving the borrower on the loan.

- **Credit Score** - Improving your credit score can help you secure a lower interest rate and reduce your PMI rate. Both of these improvements lead to lower monthly payments and better cash flow.
- **Add Borrower** - Adding a co-borrower with a strong credit profile to your loan can help you qualify for a better interest rate and lower PMI, both of which can enhance your cash flow.
- **Remove Borrower** - If one borrower has a weaker credit profile, removing them from the loan might result in a better interest rate. This can lead to lower monthly payments and improved cash flow.
- **Loan Partner** - Partnering with someone who has a strong financial profile can help you secure better loan

terms, including lower interest rates and more favorable conditions, which ultimately enhance your cash flow.

Relationship With Lender

These cash flow improving strategies are based on your relationship with the lender or lending institution.

- **Auto Pay Loan** - Setting up automatic payments can sometimes qualify you for a slight reduction in your interest rate, directly improving your cash flow by lowering your monthly mortgage payment. It may show up also as a penalty to the interest rate if you don't use autopay for the mortgage.
- **Additional Accounts** - Maintaining additional accounts or depositing more funds with your lender might earn you a small interest rate reduction, leading to improved cash flow through lower monthly payments. This is more common with commercial loans and relationship banking.

Change Amortization

These strategies to improve your cash flow deal with changing the amortization schedule of the financing you're getting.

- **Interest Only** - An interest-only loan allows you to pay only the interest for a certain period, which significantly reduces your monthly payments. This can boost your

cash flow in the short term, though it comes with long-term risks since the principal remains unpaid. You'll need to have a solid plan to deal with the loan balance when the ballon payment date arrives.
- **Negative Amortization** - A negative amortizing loan allows you to pay less than the interest due, causing the loan balance to increase over time. This lowers your initial payments and improves short-term cash flow but increases your debt over time.
- **Rate from Loan Term** - Shortening the loan term (e.g., switching from a 30-year to a 15-year mortgage) can lower your interest rate. However, this typically increases your monthly payments, so it's more about long-term savings than immediate cash flow improvement.
- **Loan Term** - Extending the loan term (e.g., from 30 to 40 years) reduces the monthly payment amount, which can improve your cash flow. However, this means you'll pay more interest over the life of the loan.

Loan Terms

These cash flow improving strategies deal with the terms (details) of the loan itself.

- **Amount Borrowed** - Putting more money down reduces the amount you need to borrow, leading to lower monthly payments. This can improve your cash flow, though it also means tying up more capital in the property.

© 2024 James Orr. All rights reserved.

- **Loan-To-Value** - A lower loan-to-value (LTV) ratio, achieved by making a larger down payment, often results in a better interest rate. This lowers your monthly payments and improves cash flow. Not only can putting more down improve your LTV and give you a better interest rate, but it might also reduce your Private Mortgage Insurance (PMI) payment since that's part of the calculation for determining PMI amounts.
- **Adjustable Rate** - An adjustable-rate mortgage (ARM) typically starts with a lower interest rate than a fixed-rate mortgage. This can enhance your cash flow in the initial years, though the rate—and your payments—can increase later.

Private Mortgage Insurance (PMI)

These strategies to improve cash flow deal primarily with Private Mortgage Insurance (PMI).

What is PMI? The lender would prefer you put at least 20% down to finance a property. With 20% down they feel comfortable enough that if you don't pay as agreed they will be able to foreclose, sell the property and get all their money back after the expenses of foreclosure and sale.

You insist on putting less than 20% down.

They may reluctantly agree, but they may charge you a higher interest rate because it is a riskier loan to them. And, additionally, they may insist that you pay a third-party insurance company a fee that insures them in case you default and they're unable to foreclose and sell the property to recoup their entire investment. This third-party insurance company is Private Mortgage Insurance.

It is insurance you pay for to protect the lender in case you default on the loan.

- **Eliminate PMI** - If you can put down at least 20% of the purchase price, you can avoid PMI altogether, significantly reducing your monthly mortgage expenses and improving your cash flow.
- **Pre-Pay PMI** - Paying PMI in a lump sum upfront instead of monthly can reduce your ongoing costs, leading to better cash flow throughout the loan term.
- **Improve Credit** - Enhancing your credit score can help you secure a lower PMI rate or even eliminate PMI altogether if your LTV ratio improves, both of which contribute to better cash flow.
- **Add Borrowers** - Added a borrower to your loan typically reduces PMI and therefore improves cash flow.

Other Properties

These cash flow improving strategies rely on tapping into other properties you own.

Some of these strategies deal with making sure your cash flow is optimized for your entire portfolio (including these other properties) and not specifically to a new property you're buying.

- **Cash Out Refi to Buy/Refi** - Consider doing a cash-out refinance on another property to use the proceeds for purchasing or refinancing your current property. This can result in better overall financing terms and improved cash flow.
- **Cash Out Refi for Larger Down Payment** - If putting more down on your current property will secure a better interest rate or eliminate PMI, consider using funds from a cash-out refinance on another property. This can lower your monthly payments and improve cash flow.
- **Rate and Term Before Acquisition** - Before purchasing a new property, consider refinancing your existing properties to better terms. As you own more properties the complexity of refinancing increases significantly. Consider this a reminder to consider this before each new purchase and to make any changes to other properties now before you add a new property that further limits what you can do. This can also improve the overall cash flow on your portfolio and might also allow you to qualify for better financing on the new purchase.

Non-Traditional Financing

These are some non-traditional financing strategies for improving cash flow you might want to consider.

- **Pay Cash** - If you have sufficient funds, paying cash for a property eliminates the need for financing altogether,

which maximizes cash flow by removing monthly mortgage payments.
- **Private Financing** - Secure a loan from family or friends (private lenders) who might offer more favorable terms than traditional banks. This can lead to lower monthly payments and improved cash flow.
- **Creative Financing** - Explore options like owner financing, wrap financing, agreement for deed, lease-options, or subject to, where the seller might offer better terms than traditional lenders. These strategies can lower your mortgage payments and enhance cash flow.
- **Assumable Loan** - If the seller's existing loan has a lower interest rate than current market rates, assuming their loan can be a great way to secure better financing terms, leading to improved cash flow. This is more likely for owner-occupant loans, so this is probably limited to owner-occupant investing strategies like house hacking or Nomad™.

While optimizing your financing is crucial for improving cash flow, it's equally important to consider how your chosen real estate investing strategy can impact your returns. Let's now explore various strategies that can enhance your cash flow by refining your overall investment approach.

Improving the Real Estate Investing Strategy

Here are the cash flow improving strategies based on improving the real estate investing strategy you're opting to utilize.

- **Term** - Adjusting the duration of your lease can significantly impact your cash flow. Shorter-term rentals, such as daily, weekly, or monthly leases, often command higher rents compared to yearly leases. However, shorter terms can also lead to increased expenses, including higher vacancy rates, more frequent marketing, and potentially higher management and maintenance costs. Offering different terms, such as furnished vs. unfurnished rentals, can also cater to various market segments, like vacation rentals or boarding houses, providing opportunities to maximize income.
- **Lease-Option** - Lease-option strategies, including variations like rent-to-own (like lease-purchases and lease-options), can dramatically improve cash flow, particularly in markets where buying is significantly more expensive than renting. These arrangements typically involve collecting a non-refundable purchase deposit/option fee, which can—mathematically—appear to add hundreds of dollars per month to your cash flow. Additionally, tenants in lease-option agreements often treat the property with more care, reducing maintenance, vacancy, and management costs. This

strategy is a form of our *Deal Alchemy*™, where you trade future appreciation returns for immediate cash flow.

- **Niche** - Specializing in a specific rental market can allow you to charge premium rents by catering to unique needs. For example, you might focus on corporate rentals, traveling nurses, or student housing. By understanding and addressing the specific requirements of your niche audience, such as providing furnished units for corporate rentals or flexible leases for students, you can add value that justifies higher rental rates. The key is to determine what additional services or amenities you can offer that will attract your target market and what premium you can reasonably charge for those services.

The following cash flow improving strategies are really just variations of house hacking where you're renting out part of the property you're living in for income and to improve cash flow. However, you could utilize these strategies even when you're not living in the property.

- **Roommates** - Renting out individual bedrooms in a single-family home, or additional units in a duplex, triplex, or fourplex, can significantly increase your cash flow. This is a common house hacking strategy where you live in one part of the property and rent out the rest. For example, you might rent out spare bedrooms in your own home or lease the other units in a multi-family property. This approach allows you to maximize the rental income from a single property by utilizing every available space.

- **Rent by Bed/Bedroom** - Some properties, particularly those near colleges or universities, may lend themselves well to renting by the bedroom or even by the bed. This strategy works particularly well with student housing, where multiple tenants share a single property. By renting out each bedroom or bed individually, you can often achieve a higher overall rent compared to leasing the entire property to a single tenant.
- **Rent by Parts** - Renting out different parts of a property, such as non-conforming units in a duplex, triplex, or fourplex, can be a lucrative strategy. It's essential to check local occupancy laws to ensure compliance. This strategy can also include more unconventional setups, such as renting out RV parking spaces, tiny homes, garages, or storage units on the property. These spaces don't have to be residential; they can be rented for commercial or recreational purposes, such as storage or use of shared community amenities like a pool or recreational center.

While optimizing your real estate investing strategy can significantly boost cash flow, another powerful approach is to enhance the property itself. By making strategic improvements and modifications to your rental property, you can potentially increase its value and appeal, leading to higher rental income and improved cash flow. Let's explore some effective strategies for improving cash flow through property enhancements.

Improving the Property

Here are the cash flow improving strategies based on making improvements to the property.

- **Subdivide** - Consider subdividing your property into multiple units to increase rental income. For example, you could rent the upstairs and downstairs separately, offering tenants more privacy while still sharing common areas like heating, cooling, mail, laundry, and possibly even the kitchen or living areas. This isn't the same as converting the property into a formal duplex or triplex; instead, it's more about creating a roommate-like situation with more separation. This setup allows you to comply with local roommate laws and zoning requirements while potentially charging higher rents, as tenants may feel like they have their own space.
- **Upgrade Property** - Enhancing your property's curb appeal and overall condition can justify charging higher rents. Improvements could include landscaping, painting, adding or improving shutters, lawn care, updating the mailbox, property address numbers, or exterior lighting. These upgrades can attract higher-paying tenants and increase the property's value. This approach is also common in value-add strategies or the BRRRR method, where the goal is to improve the property to increase its rent and overall profitability.
- **Solar** - Installing solar panels and including the cost of electricity in the base rent can make your property more attractive to tenants who value energy efficiency, potentially allowing you to charge higher rents.

© 2024 James Orr. All rights reserved.

However, you should be cautious about the legal implications of charging for utilities, as this can sometimes enter a gray area. It's advisable to consult with a local attorney to ensure compliance with utility billing regulations.
- **Furnished Rental** - Offering a furnished rental can significantly increase the rent you can charge, especially if you shift your strategy to short-term or medium-term rentals, such as vacation rentals, student rentals, or corporate housing. Furnished rentals appeal to tenants looking for convenience and are often willing to pay a premium for a move-in ready home.
- **Convert Property** - Converting a single-family property into a duplex, triplex, or fourplex can increase your rental income by creating multiple rental units within the same property. This approach is especially effective if the property is already somewhat set up for such a conversion. However, it may be cost-prohibitive or even impossible if significant structural changes are required or if zoning laws restrict such conversions. Always check with your city and county regarding zoning and licensing requirements before starting any conversion work, as this can also affect the types of loans you can secure and their terms, including the loan-to-value ratio.
- **Improvement Rent** - Charging extra rent for specific property improvements can help offset the cost of upgrades while increasing your overall rental income. For example, you might charge a tenant more for installing new carpet or a fence. While you may not be able to recoup the full cost of the improvement from a single tenant, some upgrades, like a fence, can justify

higher rents with future tenants as well, allowing you to gradually recover your investment and potentially earn a return. This strategy is particularly useful for items with a long lifespan, where the cost can be spread out over multiple tenancies.

While property improvements can significantly boost your rental income, the way you market your property can be equally important for maximizing cash flow. By implementing effective marketing strategies, you can attract high-quality tenants, reduce vacancy periods, and potentially command higher rents. Let's explore some key strategies for improving cash flow through smart marketing techniques.

Marketing the Property for Rent

Here are the cash flow improving strategies to implement while you're marketing your property for rent.

- **Optimize Marketing** - Effective marketing starts with high-quality materials. Ensure that you have professional-grade photos, a 3D tour, and a video to showcase your property. These elements can significantly enhance the appeal of your listing, attracting more potential tenants. Additionally, use online marketing as well as flyers and signs strategically around the neighborhood to increase visibility. Well-designed marketing materials make your property stand

out and convey a sense of professionalism that can justify higher rent and reduce vacancy periods.
- **Maximize Exposure** - To attract the right tenants, it's crucial to advertise your property across all available platforms where tenants might be searching. This includes online rental websites, social media, and community bulletin boards. Physical advertising, such as yard signs and directional signs leading to the property, can also capture the attention of local renters. By maximizing exposure, you increase the chances of filling vacancies quickly and with quality tenants.
- **Sales Skills** - Mastering sales skills is essential for renting your property at the highest possible rate and minimizing vacancy. This includes both phone skills for initial inquiries and in-person salesmanship during property tours. Being persuasive and knowledgeable helps you connect with potential tenants, address their concerns, and highlight the property's best features, ultimately leading to faster lease agreements and better tenant retention.
- **Optimize Showings** - Preparing your property for showings is a key step in securing a lease. Ensure the property is well-lit, smells pleasant, and is clean, neat, and in good repair. First impressions matter, and a well-presented property can make the difference between a potential tenant choosing your property over another. Additionally, create a sense of scarcity by scheduling back-to-back showings and mentioning this when booking appointments. This strategy can create urgency and increase interest among prospective tenants.

While effective marketing strategies can help attract tenants and maximize rental income, it's equally important to focus on optimizing your property's financial performance during ownership. Let's explore various strategies you can implement to improve cash flow throughout your tenure as a property owner.

While Owning the Property

Here are the cash flow improving strategies to implement while you own the property.

Refi/Pay Off Loan

Managing your mortgage can be one of the most effective ways to improve cash flow and overall property profitability.

- **Refi to Extend Term** - If your loan is old enough, consider refinancing to extend the loan term. This can lower your monthly payments and—if interest rates have dropped and/or your loan-to-value has improved—potentially secure a better interest rate, improving your cash flow.
- **Refi to Improve Rate** - If interest rates have dropped since you first took out your mortgage, refinancing to a lower rate can reduce your monthly payments and save you money over the life of the loan.
- **Payoff Loan** - If you have the financial means, paying off your loan in its entirety can eliminate your mortgage payments, drastically improving your monthly cash flow and reducing financial stress.

© 2024 James Orr. All rights reserved.

Taxes

Property taxes are a significant expense for any property owner, and managing them effectively can save you money.

- **Correct Assessor** - Ensure that the county assessor has accurate information about your property's condition and characteristics. Correcting any inaccuracies can prevent overvaluation and keep your taxes in check.
- **Contest Tax Increases** - If your property taxes increase, consider contesting the increase. Successful challenges can lead to reduced tax bills and improved cash flow.
- **Vote** - Participate in local elections and vote on measures that affect property taxes. Being informed and voting appropriately can help control future tax increases.

Insurance

Insurance is essential for protecting your investment, but it's also an area where you can manage costs.

- **Shop Insurance Rates** - Regularly compare insurance rates from different providers to ensure you're getting the best deal. Competitive rates can lower your insurance costs without sacrificing coverage.
- **Insurance Coverage** - Review your property insurance policy to make sure you have the right level of coverage. Avoid overpaying for unnecessary coverage or underinsuring your property. It is not just about

minimizing this cost while sacrificing coverage; you must make sure you minimize cost while keeping a desirable level of coverage. Sacrificing coverage is short-sighted and might significantly hurt cash flow if you ever have a claim that is you opted not to cover.
- **Insured** - Adjust your insurance policy by adding or removing people as needed to optimize your rates. This can lead to lower premiums.
- **Insurance Deductible** - Consider raising your deductible to lower your insurance premium. Taking on more risk personally can reduce your monthly insurance costs. See comments about sacrificing coverage being short-sighted above.
- **Remove PMI** - Totally different type of insurance, but if your property's equity has increased sufficiently, you may be able to remove Private Mortgage Insurance (PMI). This can significantly reduce your monthly mortgage payment.

Making Payments

How you manage your payments can also impact your overall costs.

- **Discount for Autopay** - Sign up for autopay on utilities and other bills to avoid per-bill fees. Many service providers offer small discounts or waive fees for customers who enroll in autopay.
- **Discount for Early Payments** - Some service providers, such as HOA or insurance companies, offer

discounts for early payments. Paying these bills in advance can reduce your overall expenses.

Management

Whether you manage your property yourself or hire a professional, effective management is key to maintaining profitability.

- **Self-Manage** - If you choose to manage the property yourself, ensure you stay up to date with the latest laws, best practices, and compliance issues. Self-management can save on property management fees, but it often requires a significant time investment.
- **Professional Property Manager** - Shop around for a high-quality property manager who offers reasonable fees. A good property manager can maximize your rental income and minimize headaches.
- **Manage the Manager** - Even with a professional property manager, it's important to regularly review management statements for accuracy. Mistakes can happen, and catching them early can save you money.
- **Insist on Best Practices** - Ensure your property manager follows best practices, such as marketing your property early and raising rents with each lease renewal. This proactive approach can help maximize your rental income.

Maintenance

Regular maintenance is crucial for keeping your property in good condition and minimizing vacancies.

- **Maintain Property** - Regularly maintaining your property can reduce the time it spends vacant between tenants. A well-maintained property attracts tenants quickly and reduces downtime.
- **Quality Materials** - Using quality materials for maintenance and repairs may have a higher upfront cost, but it can lower the overall cost of maintenance over time by reducing the frequency of repairs and replacements.

Depreciation

Depreciation can provide significant tax benefits, and managing it strategically can enhance your investment returns.

- **Accelerate Depreciation** - Consider accelerating depreciation on your property to maximize tax benefits in the short term. This strategy can improve your cash flow by reducing your taxable income, but it should be used with careful planning to avoid potential future tax liabilities. This can be one of the larger improvements to your cash flow.

While the strategies for improving cash flow during property ownership are crucial, it's equally important to optimize your rental income while renting it. Let's explore various techniques you can implement to enhance your cash flow during the rental phase of your investment.

While Renting the Property

Here are the cash flow improving strategies to implement while you're renting the property.

Add Services

Offering additional services can increase rental income and enhance tenant satisfaction.

- **Additional Services** - Consider offering additional services such as high-speed internet, cable, or utilities for an extra fee. Tenants often value the convenience of bundled services, making this an effective way to boost your rental income. However, be sure to check local laws, as this practice may not be permitted in some areas.
- **DFY Services** - Offer done-for-you (DFY) services such as lawn care, snow removal, or house cleaning. These services can be billed as extras, appealing to tenants who prefer convenience and are willing to pay for it.

Charge Appropriately

Setting appropriate charges can maximize your rental income while offering flexibility to tenants.

- **Bill Back** - Implement bill-back strategies for utilities or HOA services, such as charging tenants for non-potable water or other shared resources. This helps to ensure that tenants are covering their fair share of costs, improving your net income.
- **Tier Rent by Credit Score** - Adjust rent based on the tenant's credit score, with higher rent for those with lower scores. This can also apply to security deposits, where tenants with better credit pay less upfront. Check with your attorney before implementing this strategy.
- **Pet Rent** - Charge additional rent for tenants with pets. Pet rent can help cover potential wear and tear caused by pets and increase your overall rental income.

Convenience Billing

Convenience billing options can make it easier for tenants to pay rent while potentially increasing your revenue.

- **Billing Frequency** - Offer more frequent billing options, such as weekly or biweekly payments, instead of the traditional monthly schedule. This can be attractive to tenants who prefer smaller, more manageable payments but can also produce more cash flow over the same period.
- **Autopay** - Here are conflicting ideas where both options may ultimately improve cash flow. Encourage tenants to enroll in autopay by offering a discount or, conversely, charge a fee for those who do not use autopay. Autopay

can reduce late payments and ensure consistent cash flow.
- **Discount On-Time Payment** - Provide a discount for tenants who pay their rent on time or early, incentivizing prompt payments and reducing the need for late payment penalties.
- **Term** - Adjust the term of rental agreements to fit different rental strategies. Consider offering daily, weekly, or short-term/vacation rentals, which can often command higher rents than traditional monthly leases.

Timing

Optimizing the timing of lease agreements and renewals can minimize vacancies and maximize rental income.

- **Notice** - Require a 60-90 day notice from tenants if they intend not to renew their lease. This provides you with ample time to market the property and secure a new tenant, reducing vacancy periods.
- **Start Early/Test Rent** - Begin marketing the property early, even before the current tenant moves out, and start with a higher rent to test the market. This strategy allows you to adjust pricing based on demand and secure the best possible rental rate.
- **Renew Peak Season** - Align lease renewal dates to end during peak rental seasons, such as spring or summer, when demand is higher. This increases the likelihood of filling the property quickly and possibly at a higher rent.

Miscellaneous

Implementing additional requirements can protect your property and reduce potential liabilities.

- **Renter's Insurance** - Require tenants to carry renter's insurance. This protects both you and the tenant in case of damage to the property or loss of personal belongings, reducing potential conflicts and liabilities.

Conclusion

This guide has explored 94 ways to improve cash flow on rental properties across seven distinct stages of your real estate investing process.

Each stage presents unique opportunities to boost your investment's financial performance, and the cumulative effect of applying these strategies can significantly increase your property's profitability.

By focusing on cash flow improvement at every stage, you can:

- Build a more resilient and profitable real estate portfolio
- Enhance property values—especially for properties where value is driven by the income they generate, such as commercial properties
- Strengthen your ability to secure favorable financing by improving loan-to-value (LTV) and debt service coverage ratios
- Optimize tax benefits

- Accelerate savings for larger down payments and quickly replenish reserves
- Increase tenant satisfaction by enhancing the tenant experience, improving retention rates, and reducing turnover costs

Remember, even small adjustments across multiple areas can compound into substantial gains in your overall returns and financial stability.

Make it a habit to regularly review and implement these strategies, tailoring them to fit your specific properties and market conditions.

With consistent effort and strategic application, you can transform your rental properties into powerful, cash-generating assets that support your long-term financial goals.

Introduction to Monte Carlo Analysis of Rental Properties

There's a problem with how we've been modeling our investments so far. It is not unique to us. Almost everyone does it wrong.

But, we're going to fix it now.

The issue is the assumptions we've been using and how the real world works.

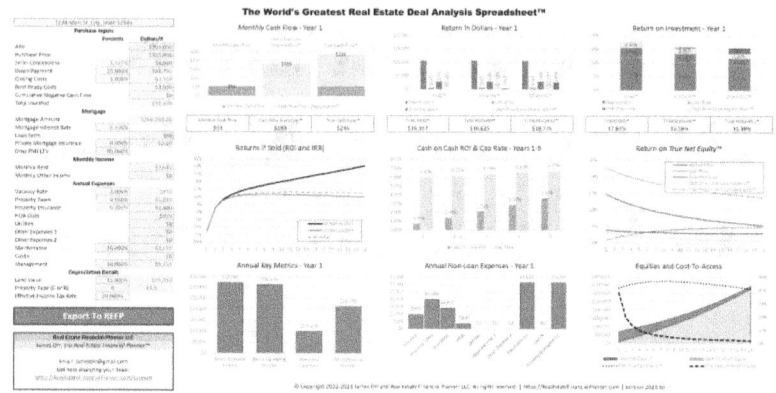

For the analysis we've been doing with *The World's Greatest Real Estate Deal Analysis Spreadsheet*™ (TWGREDAS)—and any other real estate deal analysis spreadsheet—we've used static assumptions.

We might assume that property values are going up by 3% per year. Well, that's not truly a correct representation of reality.

Heck, with the overrides tab in TWGREDAS we may have said, they go up by 3% for the first 3 years and then only 2% thereafter. Better, but still not reality.

The truth is: we really don't know how much property values will go up as we hold the property. They could go up by 3%. They could go down by 3%. They could go up then down or down then up. Could be more or less than 3%. Might be 3.1% or 2.9%. Might be up or down 6% or 10%.

If we look back at history (and we do when we consider the risks of investing in real estate), we can see what property appreciation has done over the last 100 years.

Risk Matrix: Appreciation

Likelihood	Severity				
	0 Increase	1 Small Decline	2 Medium Decline	3 Large Decline	4 Catastrophic
1	>10% Increase 7.7%			10-15% Decline 6.0%	>15% Decline 0.0%
2	5-10% Increase 15.0%		5-10% Decline 12.8%		
3	0-5% Increase 25.6%	0-5% Decline 34.6%			

© Copright 2024 James Orr and Real Estate Financial Planner LLC. All right reserved. | https://REFP.com

So, to correctly model how our investment might perform, we should not use a static 3% per year—or whatever static number you believe to be true—for property appreciation.

Our crystal balls are broken. We can't accurately predict—exactly—what appreciation will be for our properties.

We can guess. Based on what has happened in the past they will average about 3% per year.

But they may:

- Increase in value by more than 10% for the year about 7.7% of the time
- Increase between 5% and 10% for the year about 15% of the time
- Increase between 0% and 5% for the year about 25.6% of the time
- Go down in value between 0% and 5% for the year about 34.6% of the time

© 2024 James Orr. All rights reserved.

- Go down in value between 5% and 10% for the year about 12.8% of the time
- Go down in value between 10% and 15% for the year about 6% of the time

These are based on what has happened over the last 100 years. Could the future be different? Absolutely.

But it is much more accurate than just assuming that they will be going up in value by 3% per year every year.

Not Just Property Appreciation

As you probably guessed, this isn't just an issue with property appreciation. It applies to other assumptions we have as well.

Here's a list of some of the more significant ones:

- **Property Appreciation Rate** - This is the one we've been talking about already. It is how much properties go up or down in value.
- **Rent Appreciation Rate** - This is how much rents increase or decrease with each lease renewal.
- **Inflation Rate** - Inflation reflects the overall increase in prices and the decrease in purchasing power over time. It impacts everything from the cost of goods and services to the value of money itself. In the context of your portfolio, inflation affects how much your money will be worth in the future, influencing the real returns on your investments. For instance, even if your rental

income and property values rise, high inflation could erode those gains in terms of actual purchasing power. A million dollars today isn't the same as a million dollars 50 years ago and it won't be the same as a million dollars 50 years from now.
- **Mortgage Interest Rates** - Mortgage Interest Rates - Mortgage rates fluctuate over time. The rate you secure for your current property purchase or refinance won't necessarily be the same for properties you buy in one, five, or more years from now.
- **Stock Market Rate of Return** - This is how much you're earning on money you have invested in the stock market. This also applies to other investments you might have like savings accounts, bonds, CDs, cryptocurrencies, etc.

If you really want to go to freaky town, you could also model this with changing tax rates, insurance rates, maintenance and capital expenses on the property.

Does This Even Matter?

Does this even matter and why should I care?

Let's start with a simple example of someone who invests in stocks. They don't even buy a home to live in; they rent instead.

They invest approximately 10% of their income in the stock market earning 8% per year.

Using static assumptions, we could calculate that they would be financially independent (FI) after about 53.25 years.

See **Error! Reference source not found.** at the end of the chapter. We moved the charts to the end of the chapter—instead of inline—so we could show you larger, readable versions of the charts.

But what if we used a reasonable range of values for the return from the stock market instead of always 8% every year?

We could use a range of values that better approximates what the stock markets has done historically—still averaging about 8% for this selection of stocks.

Instead of seeing a smooth line showing their journey toward financial independence as shown in Error! Reference source not found. at the end of the chapter.

We'd instead see a less smooth line representing how the stock market returns change each month like Error! Reference source not found..

And, if we ran it 10 times, you'd see that when they actually achieve financial independence (when the line crosses the horizontal dotted line) is a little different each time. See Error! Reference source not found..

If the stock market performs well, they're financially independent earlier. If the stock market does not perform as well, they end up being financially independent later.

If we ran this 1,000 times and summarized the results, we can see the range of when they're financially independent. See Error! Reference source not found..

Monte Carlo Modeling

This type of analysis is called Monte Carlo modeling.

Monte Carlo modeling is a statistical technique used to simulate multiple potential outcomes for an investment or financial scenario.

It works by:

- Running hundreds or thousands of simulations with varying input parameters
- Analyzing the range and probability of different outcomes
- Providing a more nuanced understanding of potential risks and returns

For real estate investing, Monte Carlo analysis involves varying input factors such as property appreciation rates, rent increases, mortgage interest rates, inflation, and market returns. This approach allows you to better assess the likelihood of achieving your financial goals and understand the potential risks associated with your investment strategies.

I like to call it *Alternate Universe Modeling*™ because we're consider how your investments might perform if you were living in alternate universes with different futures.

© 2024 James Orr. All rights reserved.

Back to our example with someone just investing in stocks.

In Error! Reference source not found. at the end of the chapter:

- The light blue band shows the full range of results from the very worst to the very best.
- The darker blue band in the middle shows you the middle 50% of all runs. Half of the time the results are this darker band.
- The dark link at the very center shows you the median value. Half the values are higher than this. Half the values are lower than this.

If we look at the median line we can see that half the time they're financially independent around 58 years. Half the time it is after 58 years.

It could have been as early as year 48. And, it could take longer than 60 years—when we stopped modeling for this example. In fact, only about 85% of the 1,000 runs we ran were financially independent 60 years from when they started.

We can summarize this is a different chart and show what percentage of the 1,000 runs were financially independent in each month. That's Error! Reference source not found..

By using a range of values for things like the stock market rate of return, we get a much more nuanced understanding of what is likely to happen.

What If They Became Homeowners Instead of Renting?

Our last example they were renting a property to live in and investing in stocks.

What if they bought on owner-occupant property with 5% down to live in and invested in stocks?

If we used static assumptions they would be financially independent about 15 and half years faster as shown in Error! Reference source not found. at the end of the chapter.

Part of what gets them to financial independence faster is that they end up paying off their owner-occupant property 30 years after they buy it. Without a mortgage payment the threshold for them being financially independent is a little lower.

There's a little more to this story, but I don't want to go off into the weeds here. The punchline is they achieve financial independence faster with static assumptions as you can see in Error! Reference source not found..

Let's vary the property appreciation rate, mortgage interest rate, inflation rate, and stock market rate of return. If we were discussing rentals, we'd vary the rent appreciation rate as well but in this case they're not buying any rentals; we'll get to that shortly.

With variable property appreciation rates, mortgage interest rates until they lock in a 30-year fixed rate financing loan, inflation rate and stock market rate of return it looks like Error! Reference source not found..

They're financially independent as early as 33.75 years from when they start. In 99.5% of the 1,000 runs they're financially independent by the time we stop modeling at 60 years.

How does this compare to them just investing in stocks? Let's show both on one chart in Error! Reference source not found..

Buying an owner-occupant property seems to make a pretty big difference.

If we just look at what percentage of the 1,000 runs they achieve financial independence, you can see that buying the owner-occupant property is more probable (higher percentage of the runs achieve it) and they're financially independent earlier (it happens more to the left on the chart). See Error! Reference source not found..

Buying Rental Properties with 20% Down Payments

Let's assume, for now, that they don't buy an owner-occupant property with 5% down. Instead, they decide to buy 20% down rental properties as their primary investing strategy.

Any additional money beyond what they need for the rentals is still investing in stocks, but whenever they get enough for a 20% down payment they buy a rental property with very modest cash flow.

They're willing to buy up to ten 20% down payment rentals.

If we have **static assumptions** for property appreciation, rent appreciation, inflation, mortgage interest rates and the stock market rate of return, they might be financially independent after 31 years.

With static assumptions, that's about 18.67 years faster than just investing in stocks and about 3 years faster than buying an owner-occupant property and investing stocks as shown in Error! Reference source not found..

With static assumptions, they achieve financial independence faster. See Error! Reference source not found..

And, still looking at the chart above, they appear have a lot more income coming then just investing in stocks the longer they hold the rental properties.

In fact, they're earning about twice what they need to be financially independent about 48.5 years in. That means they're earning twice what they need to be financially independent before just investing in stocks as a renter is even earning enough for them to financially independent at all.

© 2024 James Orr. All rights reserved.

Not long after they achieve financial independence just investing in stocks as a renter, they're earning 3 times what they need to be financially independent with their 10 rentals.

But, this is about Monte Carlo modeling, so what if we did vary property appreciation rates, rent appreciation rates, inflation, mortgage interest rates and the stock market rate of return?

It is important to realize that because the property prices vary with each run sometimes the properties they're buying can be slightly more or less expensive. On average though, property prices are going up at about 3% per year.

Rent is similar. Rents can go up or down, but overall, rents are increasing by about 3% per year.

Mortgage interest rates started at about 8.5% for a non-owner-occupant loan without paying significant points. But, mortgage interest rates can get better—or worse—over time as they're acquiring properties. That means sometimes properties will cash flow better and sometimes they'll cash flow a little worse.

Let's look at their journey to financial independence buying ten 20% down payment rentals in Error! Reference source not found..

You can see there are times when the market goes in their favor (both the real estate and stock market) they achieve financial independence early. And, there are times when they still don't quite achieve it through 60 years.

© 2024 James Orr. All rights reserved.

How does it compare to the two previous strategies: renting and investing exclusively in stocks and buying an owner-occupant property and exclusively investing in stocks? See Error! Reference source not found..

It is getting harder to see what is happening in the chart as we add additional comparisons.

We can make it easier in two different ways. First, we can look at the same chart, but turn off the shaded areas for each strategy.

This would leave just the median—or the middle-most result—where half of them are better and half are worse. That's Error! Reference source not found..

This chart doesn't show up the range of results (how early or late they achieve FI) but it does show how much more they're likely to earn by buying the rentals by what percent of their financial independence goal they're earning.

By earning a higher percentage of the amount they need to be financially independent, they're able to support a higher standard of living.

In other words, if they needed to be earning $10,000 per month passively to be considered financially independent, but their earning 200% of that—or $20,000 per month—they could live at a much higher standard of living on $20,000 per month than the $10,000 per month that they needed—at a minimum—to be considered financially independent.

The second way to make it easier to see what is happening is looking at the percentage of the 1,000 runs that achieved financial independence like we did previously. That's Error! Reference source not found..

Buying ten 20% down payment rentals sees them achieving financial independence earlier (more left on the chart above) and then has a similar success rate to what they'd see if they bought an owner-occupant and invested in stocks.

Owner-Occupant, Rentals and Stocks

I think you know what's coming next: what if they bought an owner-occupant property with 5% down, then bought up to nine more rental properties, each with 20% down payments and invested the rest in stocks?

With static assumptions that's about 3.5 years faster than just renting and buying ten 20% down payment rentals. See Error! Reference source not found..

If we do Monte Carlo modeling, it looks like Error! Reference source not found..

Doing a very busy version of this chart by comparing it to the other strategies so far, it looks like Error! Reference source not found..

If we just look at the 50th percentile (median) value for the four options as seen in Error! Reference source not found..

It shows that buying the owner-occupant property and nine 20% down payment rentals appears to be faster and gives them a higher standard of living than even buying ten 20% down payment rentals.

If we look at the percentage of the 1,000 runs for reach strategy that achieved financial independence and when, we can see that buying an owner-occupant property and then nine 20% down rentals is the best performer yet as seen in Error! Reference source not found..

In the chart above you can see that not only does financial independence tend to happen faster (a little to the left on the chart), it also tends to be more consistent (a higher percentage of the runs achieve FI).

Nomad™ Real Estate Investing Strategy Example

There's so much more we could do with this, but for now I'll wrap it up with a slight curve ball.

Instead of buying an owner-occupant property and then buying nine 20% down payment rentals, let's imagine they Nomad™.

- They buy an owner-occupant property with 5% down payment.
- They live there for *at least* a year. That's a requirement of the lender to get an owner-occupant loan with an owner-occupant down payment and owner-occupant mortgage interest rate.

© 2024 James Orr. All rights reserved.

- Once their year is up AND they've saved up enough for another 5% down payment, they buy another owner-occupant property and move into it.
- They take the previous property they were living in and convert it to a rental property
- They repeat this until they have 9 rentals and the property they're living in

Instead of having to save up for 20% down payments, they acquire the same nine rental properties with only 5% down on each by moving into each one as an owner-occupant.

Is this better? Is this more probable for them to be financially independent? Is this faster to financial independence? Does this give a higher standard of living than the other strategies so far? And—we won't cover it here because it is a longer discussion—but is it more or less risky?

It turns out that with static assumptions (not Monte Carlo modeling yet), Nomad™ is 58 months (almost 5 years) faster to financial independence. See Error! Reference source not found..

If we add variability and do Monte Carlo modeling, we can look at how the Nomad™ strategy performs in Error! Reference source not found..

Brace yourself for the busy version comparing them all at the same time in Error! Reference source not found..

And, if we turn off the range of results and just look at the middle most (median) of the 1,000 runs for each strategy, we can see the following in Error! Reference source not found..

Still a bit busy to see what is going on, but I will point out, in the chart above, the Nomad™ strategy seems to give them the fastest achievement of financial independence and highest standard of living.

Isn't it interesting.

If we look at the percentage of the 1,000 runs that achieve financial independence and by when you can see even better in Error! Reference source not found..

The Nomad™ strategy achieves financial independence earliest (to the left on the chart above). It also has a higher probability of being financially independent earlier.

Additional Modeling

Now that we know the importance of considering the variability that might occur in the future, this is really just the beginning.

There is a ridiculous amount more to dig into here. We've just barely scratched the surface.

There's a lot more to model.

For example, we could model each strategy you're considering seeing how each strategy performs:

- Buying long-term buy and hold rental properties (short-term rentals, medium-term rentals, student rentals, storage units, assisted living, apartments, etc)

© 2024 James Orr. All rights reserved.

- Buying properties utilizing creative financing (owner financing, wrap financing, loan assumptions, rent-to-owns, agreements for deed, subject-to)
- Variations on the Nomad™ strategy (Nomad™ by Proxy, Nomad™ with House Hacking, Nomad™ to Short-Term Rental, Nomad™ with Lease-Option Exits, *The Ultimate Real Estate Agent Retirement Plan*™)
- House Hacking and related strategies
- Short-Term Rentals and related strategies
- Flipping properties and related strategies
- BRRRR and related strategies
- And much, much more

Or, combining one or more of these strategies at the same time (fix and flipping while acquiring long-term or short-term rentals as an example) or sequentially (fix and flipping for 10 years then switch to buy and hold).

Or, we could test a wide assortment of variations to your strategy:

- More or less reserves (and its impact on both speed and risk)
- More or less down payment size up to buying properties for all cash
- Buying down interest rates or not
- Getting roommates or not (house hacking)
- Selling via lease-options versus with a real estate agent or for sale by owner
- Paying off properties early with extra cash flow versus not

© 2024 James Orr. All rights reserved.

- Doing cash out refinances to buy additional properties faster
- Buying properties and selling them when you could take the proceeds (after all expenses including taxes) and then investing that money in stocks, bonds or something else to be financially independent
- Buying more properties than you need and selling them to pay off properties when it means you'd be financially independent
- And much, much more

Not Just Financial Independence

When we do these models, it is important to consider more than just how fast you're able to get to financial independence—even though that's what we focused on here.

Sometimes it is about your standard of living once you are financially independent. Some strategies might just barely get you to your minimum required income to be financially independent. While others will give you far more each month than you initially stated you needed allowing you to live at a much higher standard of living than you originally required.

Sometimes, it is about measuring, comparing and ultimately minimizing risks. Some strategies are riskier than others. They might get you to financial independence, on average, 1 year faster, but there's a 20 times greater chance you'll run out of money by pursuing that strategy than another one that gets you to financial independence, on average, a year slower.

That all might be worth considering... especially for your own unique situation.

It is important for you to evaluate your own strategy utilizing Monte Carlo modeling to better understand how to achieve financial independence faster, easier, with higher probability of success, with a higher standard of living and with less overall risk.

Or, if you are going to ignore one or more of those things, deliberately and strategically choosing to ignore them with full knowledge of the consequences.

Figure 1

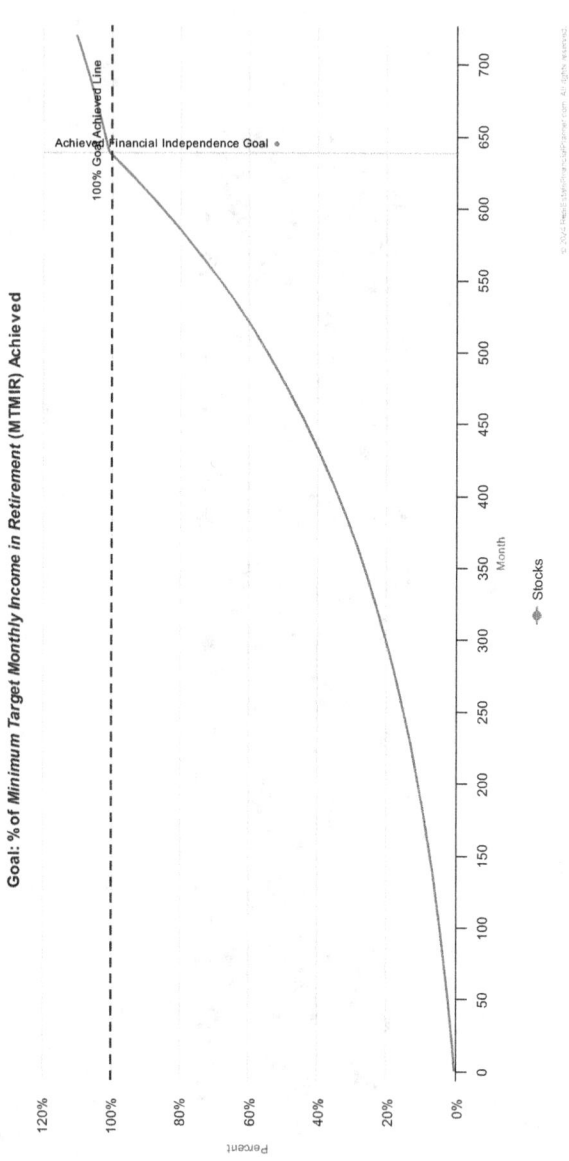

Figure 2

© 2024 James Orr. All rights reserved.

Figure 3

© 2024 James Orr. All rights reserved.

Figure 4

Figure 5

Figure 6

Figure 7

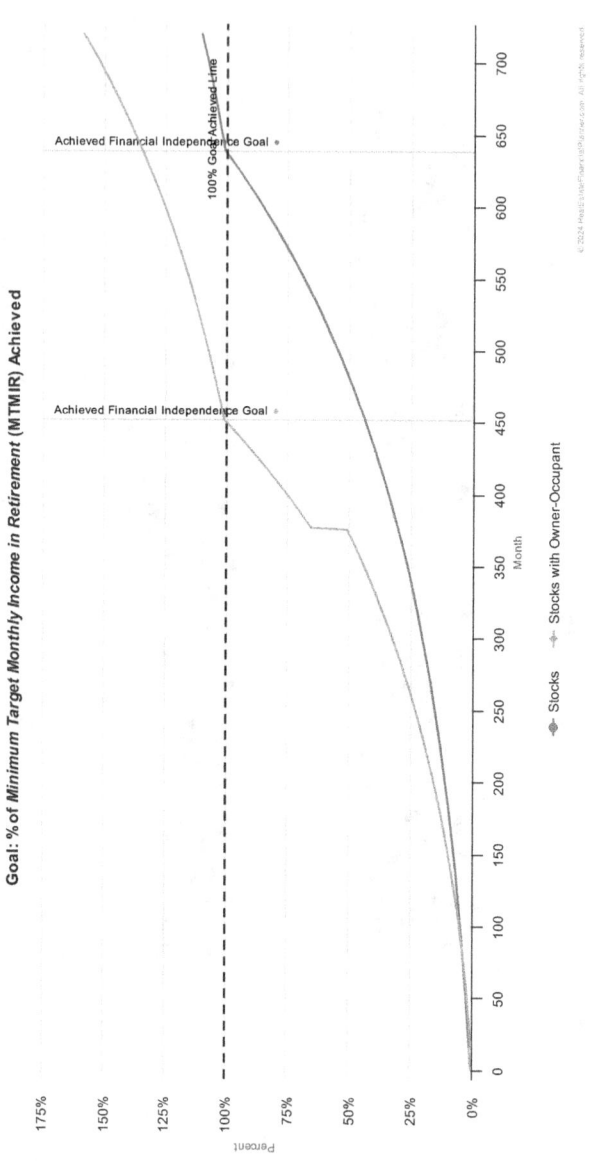

Figure 8

© 2024 James Orr. All rights reserved.

Figure 9

Figure 10

Figure 11

© 2024 James Orr. All rights reserved.

Figure 12

Figure 13

Figure 14

Figure 15

Figure 16

Figure 17

Figure 18

Figure 19

Figure 20

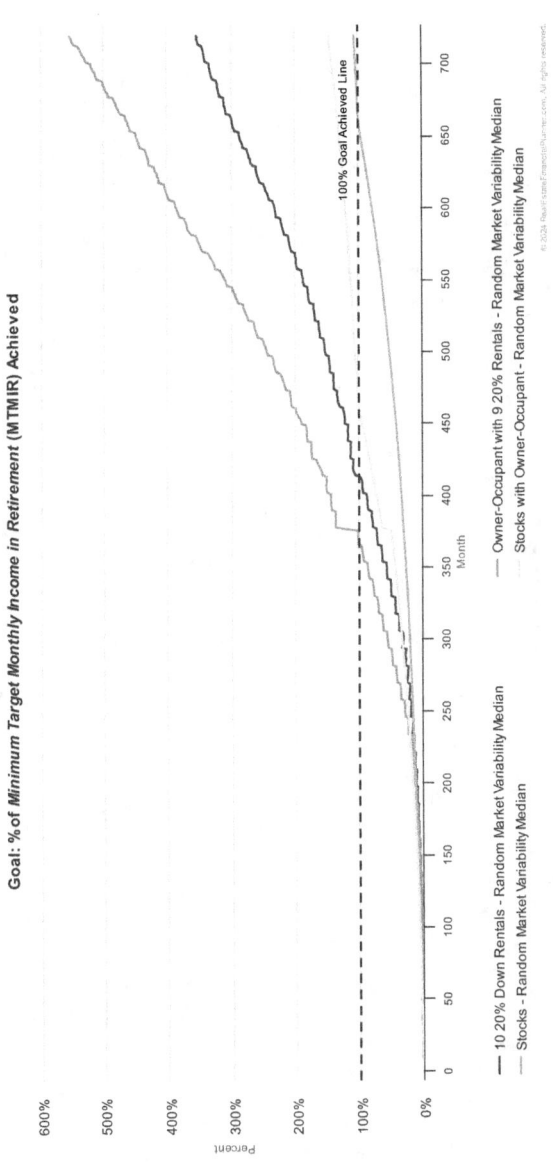

Figure 21

© 2024 James Orr. All rights reserved.

Figure 22

Figure 23

Figure 24

Figure 25

Figure 26

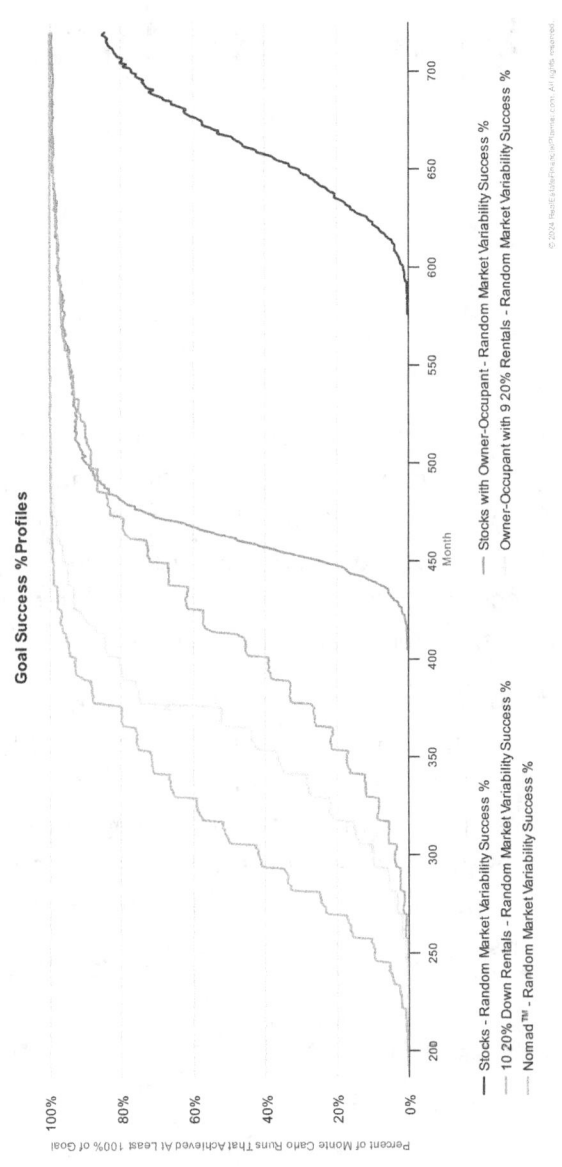

Figure 27

About the Author

James Orr is a seasoned real estate investor and the visionary creator of the Real Estate Financial Planner™ software. With a passion for sharing his wealth of knowledge, James has authored numerous books on real estate investing, covering a wide array of topics to help both novice and experienced investors succeed.

Living in Loveland, Colorado, James enjoys a fulfilling life with his wife, Tammy, whom he has been happily married to since 1995. Together, they have raised two grown sons. When he's not writing or managing his real estate investments, James is dedicated to teaching others the secrets of financial independence through smart property investments.

Also by James Orr

- The Real Estate Investing Mentor series of topic books
- How to Achieve Financial Independence and Live Your Passion Regardless of Age or Income: 10 Paths to Financial Independence Analyzed
- How to Acquire a Multi-Million Dollar Real Estate Portfolio With Just $3,000
- How to Acquire a Multi-Million Dollar Real Estate Portfolio Earning Just $5,000 Per Month
- Nomad™
- Ultimate Nomad™ Checklist
- Northern Colorado Real Estate Advisor
- Acquiring a Portfolio of Cash Flowing Properties In Northern Colorado: A Real Estate Financial Planner™ Blueprint
- Real Estate Investing Systems

Software and Spreadsheets

- Real Estate Financial Planner™ software
- The World's Greatest Real Estate Deal Analysis Spreadsheet™
- Should I Sell My Rental Property Spreadsheet™
- Should I Refinance My Rental Property Spreadsheet™
- CapEx Estimator for Rental Property – Basic and Advanced Spreadsheets
- Financial Independence Asset Allocation and Cash Flow Engines Spreadsheet™
- The Investor's Agent One-Page Business Plan™

© 2024 James Orr. All rights reserved.

A Small Request

Thank you for reading *The Real Estate Investing Mentor: The Affordable $50K Coaching Alternative* topic book on **Introduction to Flipping Properties**.

I am positive if you follow what I've written, you will be on your way to successfully investing in real estate. When you do please reach out and share your story.

I have a small, quick favor to ask. Would you mind taking a minute or two and leaving an honest review for this book on Amazon?

Reviews are the BEST way to help others purchase this book and keep the price of my books low for everyone, and I check all my reviews looking for helpful feedback.

Please visit:

https://REFP.info/intro-flipping-book

© 2024 James Orr. All rights reserved.

Questions?

Thank you for taking the time to read this book. If a concept sparked a question or if you feel there's an area that could be explained more clearly, I'd truly appreciate hearing from you. You can reach me at **jamesorr@gmail.com** with any feedback specific to this title. My goal is to make each book as helpful and practical as possible, and your input plays a big part in that.

Just a note—while I'm here to help deepen your understanding of this book's topics, this isn't intended as a personal coaching service. For advice tailored to your own situation, I encourage you to work closely with a real estate agent who can provide the insight and support unique to your goals.

Thank you again for reading, and for helping me make this series an even better resource for investors like you.

© 2024 James Orr. All rights reserved.

www.ingramcontent.com/pod-product-compliance
Lightning Source LLC
Chambersburg PA
CBHW071125240526
45465CB00024B/1243